Two
Hidden Treasures

Rachelle C. Hood

Visit our website at www.freedomlinebooks.com.

Acknowledgement

"The prisoners ... as if chained with them" Hebrews 13:3.

"His glory is like a firstborn bull, and his horns like the horns of the wild ox; together with them He shall push the peoples to the ends of the earth; they are the ten thousands of Ephraim, and they are the thousands of Manasseh."

--- Deuteronomy 33:17

"... for I am a Father to Israel, and Ephraim [Israel] is My firstborn."

--- Jeremiah 31:9

CONTENTS

Prologue

God will execute a worldwide spiritual revival in the last hours of the last days—the likes of which the world has never seen—just before His return. He will use two unusual treasures to support this movement. Both are hidden as of this writing.

The first hidden treasure is Israel (Ephraim). I am not speaking of the Jews presently residing in the land of Israel. It is a historical fact that after the death of King Solomon, God split the 12 tribes of Israel into the Northern Kingdom of Israel and the Southern Kingdom of Judah. Solomon's descent into idolatry forced the split. At the time of the separation, the tribe of Benjamin joined the tribe of Judah to create the Southern kingdom. The remaining 10 tribes formed the Northern kingdom.

Jews are descendants of the tribe of Judah and are from the Southern kingdom. (Or else, their ancestors chose or were forced to convert to Judaism at some point in history, which is the case of most Jews living in Israel today.) Mistakenly, many people speak of Jews as if they represent the whole house of Israel. They do not. Jacob had 12 sons. The 12 sons formed 12 tribes. Descendants of the other 10 are alive today.

Joseph, Jacob's favorite son through Rachel, fathered two sons in Egypt—Manasseh and Ephraim. On his deathbed, Israel (formerly Jacob) passed the right of the firstborn to his younger grandson, Ephraim. By the way, the implications of this are more sweeping than anyone has ever realized. The passing of this sacred birthright to Ephraim will play a major role in the unfolding of end-time events.

After God split Israel into two kingdoms, Ephraim grew into one of Israel's largest tribes. It occupied the northernmost part of Israel. Over the course of time, the ruling tribe of Ephraim came to represent the 10 remaining tribes of Israel and the name, Ephraim, became synonymous with Israel.

Israel, even after divided, was considered a wife to God. While both kingdoms were unfaithful to the Lord, the Northern kingdom (Ephraim) led the way in the worship of other gods. She refused to heed God's repeated warnings to put away her idols and return to Him. Since Ephraim wanted so much to be like the Gentiles around her, God scattered her to the Gentile nations in 722 B.C., where her descendants remain today. But much has occurred during the past 2,700 years!

For more than 2,000 years, many of Jacob's descendants have kept the testimony of Jesus Christ though they believe they are "Gentiles." They are hidden within in the body of Christ throughout the world. Today, they are a part of the Good Shepherd's sheepfold, following in His footsteps. They are believers in Christ, who have Hebrew roots and don't know it. But God knows *who* they are and *where* they are. At the age's end, by an unprecedented move of His Spirit, God will assemble a Hebraic army corps to ignite an end-time spiritual revival within His body. Many souls will be ushered into the kingdom of God as a result.

The second hidden treasure is crude oil that the Lord will release at a set and appointed time on His calendar. It will be a substantial financial trust, given to His body to support the massive spiritual movement that will overtake the globe. This trust was bequeathed by God to Ephraim's descendants through Jacob's double blessing on Joseph. As God's firstborn, Ephraim's descendants must manage the trust for His kingdom. The unsettling news is the oil will be released with a colossal earthquake. The massive quake will fracture large regions of the United States, where many of Ephraim's descendants are presently hidden.

PART ONE:
Ephraim...
The Hidden Treasure

Chapter 1
Who is Ephraim?

In 2002, the Lord began to reveal to me the truth about Ephraim, the 10 lost tribes of Israel's Northern kingdom. The Lord began by putting a powerful, but obscure book in my hand by Batya Wootten, *"Who is Israel? And Why You Need to Know."* The author's scholarly presentation of Old and New Testament Scriptures on the topic challenged my thinking and blew away years of casual suppositions picked up from the mainstream church and popular media.

Wooten made the indisputable case that many of Ephraim's descendants were now "a multitude in the midst of the nations" hidden within the body of Christ! They are Hebraic people of many nationalities and colors, who embraced Christ as their Messiah. *And*... they have no idea who they are!

Today, more than two billion believers comprise the body of Christ. These believers are mostly Gentiles, who have been grafted onto "The Olive Tree of Israel." Scripture teaches that Gentiles are grafted onto the olive tree as "wild branches" and have been adopted as "spiritual heirs of Abraham" receiving the "seal of righteousness of faith" (Romans 11:11-32, 4:9-12, Galatians 3:9). The God of Abraham, Isaac, and Jacob wanted the olive tree to be a witness for Him, revealing His goodness, greatness, and glory to the Gentile nations of the world.

The tree originally had two branches since God always established a matter with at least two witnesses (Deuteronomy 17:6, 19:15, John 8:17). Judah was one branch and Ephraim was the other. Both failed as faithful witnesses, so God broke off their branches (Jeremiah 11:16-17, Zechariah 4:11-14, Jeremiah 5:10-11, Revelation 11:3-4). The Apostle Paul, however, instructed that "broken branches" can be grafted back onto the olive tree if there is repentance (Romans 11:23).

A mystery kept hidden until now is that many Gentile believers are descendants of Ephraim! God foresaw Ephraim being grafted back onto the olive tree as a faithful "wild branch" when He promised the patriarchs that their descendants would be a "multitude of nations":

- God promised Abraham that his descendants would be as "numerous as the stars" (Genesis 15:5, 22:7; Exodus 32:13), and he would be the father of "many nations" or "a multitude of nations" (goyim), which meant "multitude of Gentiles" (Genesis 17:1-6).

- The promise passed from Abraham to Isaac (Genesis 26:3-4), and then to Jacob (Genesis 28:4).

- God also promised Jacob that his descendants would be "as the dust of the earth" and they would "spread abroad to the west and the east, to the north and south," and in his seed "all the families of the earth" would be blessed (Genesis 28:13-14).

- God instructed Jacob, after He changed his name to Israel, to be "fruitful and multiply." He also promised Jacob that "a nation *and* a company of nations" would proceed from him. Kings would come from his body (Genesis 35:11).

- Israel (formerly Jacob), on his deathbed, prophesied that Ephraim and Manasseh—Joseph's two sons—would grow to become "a multitude in the midst of the earth" (Genesis 48:16). He prophesied Ephraim's descendants would become "a multitude of nations" (Genesis 48:19).

In Psalm 45, a Messianic psalm that, according to Luke 24:44 Christ must fulfill, v. 14 declared: *"And she shall be brought to the King in robes of many colors."* That verse hinted at a tie between Joseph's coat of many colors and Christ's bride being composed of many nations and colors. Ephraim's descendants are a part of this colorful assembly!

Surely, Christ had Ephraim in mind when He told the Canaanite woman from the region of Tyre and Sidon: *"I was not sent except to the lost sheep of the house of Israel"* (Matthew 15:24). He was not just speaking about the Judeans of His day. He was also referring to the lost tribes that had been scattered to the Gentile nations, millennia earlier. Ultimately, through His blood sacrifice, the two houses of Israel—Ephraim and Judah—will be reunited under His headship. Even in Jesus' time, Ephraim was a "Gentile," lost within the nations of the world, completely unrecognizable by his brethren.

In Christ's quest to save Israel's lost sheep, He made a promise. He said "whosoever will" come to Him—Jew or Gentile—would not be cast out (John 6:37). By His Spirit, they would be united to His Father through Him.

Ephraim Scattered to the Nations

In 722 B.C., God sent the Assyrians to invade the Northern kingdom of Israel (Ephraim) because of her idolatry. The Lord wrote a "certificate of divorce" to His adulterous wife because she was unrepentant. Many died in the Assyrian invasion. However, many others were scattered to the nations. Since Ephraim insisted on mingling with the Gentiles, God allowed her to become one when He banished her (Hosea 4:16-19, 7:8-10).

Surprisingly, the Southern kingdom (comprised of Judah and Benjamin), followed in the footsteps of Ephraim/Israel:

> *... Have you seen what backsliding Israel has done? She has gone up on every high mountain and under every green tree, and there played the harlot. And I said, after she had done all these things, "Return to Me." But, she did not return. And her treacherous sister Judah saw it. Then I saw that for all the causes for which backsliding Israel had committed adultery, I had put her away and given her a certificate of divorce; yet her treacherous sister Judah did not hear, but went and played the harlot also (Jeremiah 3:6-9).*

However, God did not abandon Judah for the same sins for which He abandoned Israel/Ephraim because of His covenant with His servant David (Isaiah 50:1). Instead, Judah went into Babylonian exile for 70 years. There would be a time of separation only, because God promised He would establish David's dynasty forever:

> *When your days are over and you rest with your fathers, I will raise up your offspring to succeed you, who will come from your own body, and I will establish his kingdom. He is the one who will build a house for My Name, and I will establish the throne of his kingdom forever. I will be his Father, and he will be My son ... Your house and your kingdom will endure forever before Me; your throne will be established forever (2 Samuel 7:12-14, 16, NIV).*

A remnant of Jews returned to Jerusalem after the Babylonian exile. But in 70 A.D., God scattered Judah to the nations, just as He did Ephraim several millennia earlier. Judah's dispersion was because she rejected Christ as her Messiah.

Ephraim's Ordained Return

The Lord sent an "east wind" to carry Ephraim away (Hosea 13:15-16), but in the latter days He promised He would gather Ephraim's descendants. *"They shall come trembling from the west; they shall come trembling like a bird from Egypt"* (Hosea 11:10-11, NIV). God promised that He would save "the outcasts of Israel" (Isaiah 11:12) "from afar" and "from the land of their captivity" (Jeremiah 30:10). He would not make a full end of His heritage (Jeremiah 30:11) but purge the rebels from among her (Ezekiel 20:38).

God knew when He sowed Ephraim to the nations that hundreds of centuries of brutal oppression in exile would turn her heart back to Him (Hosea 2:23, Zechariah 10:9-12). He knew the sowing would one day produce a righteous harvest for His glory. The name Ephraim means "fruitful." In fact, Joseph named his second son Ephraim because God made him fruitful in Egypt, the land of his captivity.

After being severely chastened, God declared Ephraim would repent. They would seek after Him with all their heart, and in His mercy, He would raise them up and restore them to Himself. Ephraim would produce fruit for Him after all:

- *They will come with weeping [in penitence and for joy], pouring out prayers [for the future]. I will lead them back; I will cause them to walk by streams of water and bring them in a straight way in which they will not stumble, for I am a Father to Israel, and Ephraim [Israel] is My firstborn (Jeremiah 31:9, Amplified Bible).*

- *I have surely heard Ephraim bemoaning himself: "You have chastised me, and I was chastised, like an untrained bull; restore me, and I will return, for You are the Lord of my God. Surely, after my turning, I repented; and after I was instructed, I struck myself on the thigh; I was ashamed, yes, even humiliated, because I bore the reproach of my youth." Is Ephraim My dear son? Is he a pleasant child? For though I spoke against him, I earnestly remember him still. Therefore, My heart yearns for him; I will surely have mercy on him, says the Lord (Jeremiah 31:18-20).*

- *Come, and let us return to the Lord; for He has torn, but He will heal us; He has stricken, but He will bind us up. After two days He will revive us; on the third day He will raise us up, that we may live in His sight. Let us know. Let us pursue the knowledge of the Lord (Hosea 6:1-3a).*

- *Ephraim will say, "What have I to do anymore with idols?" I have heard and observed him. I am like a green cypress tree; your fruit is found in Me" (Hosea 14:8).*

- *... I will save the house of Joseph. I will bring them back, because I have mercy on them. They shall be as though I had not cast them aside; for I am the Lord their God, and I will hear them. Those of Ephraim shall be like a mighty man, and their heart shall rejoice as if with wine. Yes, their children shall see it and be glad; their heart will rejoice in the Lord. I will whistle for them and gather them, for I will redeem them; and they shall increase as they once increased (Zechariah 10:6-8).*

Ephraim—A Restored "Fruitful" Witness

It should not amaze us that God accomplished exactly what He set out to do from the beginning. He used Jacob's seed, Ephraim, to help preserve His testimony in the earth for the past 2,000 years!

Today, Ephraim's descendants—immersed in Gentile cultures throughout the world—praise, worship, and adore Christ as Messiah. Ephraim has become the restored wife God said Israel would be (Hosea 2:16-17, Hosea 2:19-20, Jeremiah 3:12-15). Through Christ's shed blood, God has written His law on Ephraim's heart. He will also write it on Judah's heart at the set and appointed time in the future:

> *Behold the days are coming, says the Lord, when I will make a New Covenant with the house of Israel and with the house of Judah. ... I will put My law within them and on their hearts will I write it; and I will be their God, and they will be My people (Jeremiah 31:31-34).*

Speaking of the whole house of Israel, God said through the Prophet Ezekiel: *"I will make you pass under the rod, and I will bring you into the bond of the covenant; I will purge the rebels from among you, and those who transgress Me ...." (Ezekiel 20:37-38).*

While Ephraim's descendants do not yet know who they are, rest assured, God does. He has called them to be His witnesses in the nations, where they were scattered:

> *You are my witnesses, says the Lord, and My servant whom I have chosen, that you may know Me, believe Me and remain steadfast to Me, and understand that I am He. Before Me there was no God formed, neither shall there be after Me. I, even I, am the Lord, and besides Me there is no Savior ... I have declared [the future] and have saved ... therefore, you are My witnesses, says the Lord, that I am God (Isaiah 43:10-13, Amplified Bible).*

Ephraim is now a part of Christ's body, hidden in her, and as God's firstborn, these descendants of Jacob shall be the great witnesses God always intended Jacob's seed to be. As part of Christ's bride, Ephraim shall help lead His body during the most turbulent period the Church, Israel, or the world has ever seen. Many of Ephraim's descendants will sparkle like stars and shine brightly in the great darkness of the Tribulation:

> *At that time Michael shall stand up, the great prince who stands watch over the sons of your people; and there shall be a time of trouble, such as never was since there was a nation, even to that time. And at that time your people shall be delivered, everyone who is found written in the book. And many of those who sleep in the dust of the earth shall awake, some to everlasting life, some to shame and everlasting contempt. Those who are wise shall shine like the brightness of the firmament (stars), and those who turn many to righteousness like the stars forever and ever (Daniel 12:1-3).*

Judah—God's Second Witness

The God of Israel always establishes a matter with two witnesses. He needed two messengers for His twofold communiqué to mankind. His bountiful grace was only half of the transmission. For more than 2,000 years, our heavenly Father has used Ephraim, throughout the world, to help preserve His testimony of salvation by grace.

God also has a Law. As physical and spiritual heirs of Adam and Eve, we have all broken it. Eternal death is the punishment for lawbreakers. For more than 2,500 years, the Father has used Judah (Jews)—many converts to the faith—as a witness to His Law.

The Law is as important as grace. It brought us to Christ (Galatians 3:24). So, although rejecting Christ as Messiah, the Jews have been faithful to keep, honor, and safeguard God's Torah (Law) since her release from Babylonian captivity. Most encouragingly, Scripture reveals a remnant of Judah (Jews) will emerge as powerful evangelists for Christ during the Tribulation: *"And I heard the number of those sealed. One hundred and forty-four thousand of all the tribes of the children of Israel were sealed: of the tribe of Judah twelve thousand were sealed...."* (Revelation 7:4-5).

Clearly, it is God's desire to reunite into one house, a divided Israel, under His New Covenant, sealed by the blood of the Lamb. All signs point to this unprecedented reunification taking place in our generation!

Chapter 2
The Mystery of the Hidden Treasure

Throughout the ages, Satan has sought to annihilate God's chosen people. However, using what Satan intended for destruction, God furthered His own glorious purposes. It is true when Ephraim turned to other lovers (idols), God banished her. And when Judah rejected her Messiah, God dispersed her among the nations.

But ...

God never lost track of His people. He hid vast numbers of Jacob's descendants from Satan, the world, and themselves. He knew, in time, He would win many to Himself to proclaim His glory. Scripture describes Israel as God's special treasure in the earth (Exodus 19:5, Psalm 135:4). In these last days, Jacob's *lost* progeny has become the Lord's *hidden* treasure.

In Matthew 13, Christ shared with his disciples seven mysteries (parables) about the kingdom of heaven. Most people misinterpret the fifth and sixth mysteries—the Parable of the Hidden Treasure and the Parable of the Pearl of Great Price.

The Parable of the Hidden Treasure is: *"Again, the kingdom of heaven is like a treasure hidden in a field, which a man found and hid, and for the joy over it he goes and sells all that he has and buys that field" (Matthew 13:44).*

The Parable of the Pearl of Great Price follows: *"Again, the kingdom of heaven is like a merchant seeking beautiful pearls, who when he had found one pearl of great price, went and sold all that he had and bought it" (Matthew 13:45-46).*

A cursory reading of the parables might lead one to think both mysteries picture salvation as the treasured possession—the hidden treasure and pearl of great price. At a glance, they appear to suggest salvation through Christ is considered so valuable that when people discover it, they eagerly sell everything they must to possess it.

While salvation is, indeed, an unrivaled treasure, this is not what the parables illustrate. Salvation cannot be purchased. It is a free gift. Neither Christ, nor His gospel is for sale.

Israel (Ephraim)—The Hidden Treasure

In Parable of the Hidden Treasure, the field represents the world, just as the field represents the world in the Parable of the Wheat and Tares (Matthew 13:37). Believers in Christ are not to "buy the world." They, instead, are encouraged to give it up, let it go in exchange for a heavenly citizenship.

Further, in this parable, the man is Christ, just as the man is Christ in the wheat-tares parable (Matthew 13:37). The hidden treasure is Israel! Christ (man) gives up everything to buy or redeem the world (field) that hides the hidden treasure (Israel).

Careful study of Scripture shows only Israel has ever been referred to as a special (or peculiar) treasure to the Lord:

- *I bore you on eagles' wings and brought you to Myself. Now, therefore, if you will indeed obey My voice and keep My Covenant, then you shall be a special treasure to Me above all people; for all the earth is Mine. And you shall be to Me a kingdom of priests and a holy nation (Exodus 19:4-6).*

- *For you are a holy people to the Lord your God; the Lord your God has chosen you to be a people for Himself, a special treasure above all the peoples on the face of the earth (Deuteronomy 7:6 and 14:2).*

- *For the Lord has chosen Jacob for Himself, Israel for His special treasure (Psalms 135:4).*

Finding the Treasure ...

In the Garden of Eden, Satan usurped dominion over the earth from Adam and Eve. When he did, he became prince of this world (John 12:31, 14:30, 2 Corinthians 4:4). That is why Satan could offer Christ the earth's kingdoms in the desert wilderness (Luke 4:5-7).

Around 2100 B.C., God established a covenant with Abraham, inaugurating him Father of the Faith. The Lord promised to make his descendants as "numerous as the stars." The promise passed from Abraham to Isaac and from Isaac to Jacob.

Jacob, who was later named Israel, fathered 12 sons. The 12 sons eventually formed the 12 tribes of Israel. At the set time, God freed the children of Israel from Egyptian bondage. That was the point where He established or "found" Israel as His special treasure above all the people of the earth.

Hiding the Treasure ...

In 722 B.C., the Northern kingdom of Israel (Ephraim) was sown to the nations by the Assyrians. Consequently, Ephraim's descendants have remained hidden in Gentile territories for more than 2,700 years! They were absorbed within the nations.

Roughly 100 years after Christ's death, God used the Romans to disperse the Southern kingdom of Judah throughout the nations of the world. Despite persecution, they multiplied where they were scattered. (Special Note: After Israel was reestablished as a nation in 1948, the Lord began gathering converts to Judaism and descendants of Judah from all parts of the world. However, Ephraim's descendants, for the most part, have remained hidden.)

Buying the Field ...

But for the joy set before him, the man (Christ) purchased (redeemed) the field (world). Christ purchased the world when He went to the cross. Earth's title deed transferred to Him from Satan, the usurper. His blood sacrifice secured the hidden treasure—a people formed and set apart for God's special purposes in the earth: *"This people I have formed for Myself; they shall declare My praise"* (Isaiah 43:21). It was always God's intent that His peculiar treasure be a holy people unto Himself, to serve Him as priests, representing Him to the nations and the nations to Him. The treasure would become a part of His bride.

The Church—The Precious Pearl of Great Price

The Church, the body of Christ, is the "one pearl of great price" that the merchant (Christ) sold everything He possessed to purchase (Acts 20:28, 1 Corinthians 6:20, 2 Corinthians 8:9, Ephesians 5:25). And just as pearls are formed in oysters over a long period of time by accretion, the Church has been forming the same way for the past 2,000 years. The Church is the Bridegroom's precious bride. And within her is His special, peculiar, hidden treasure—Israel/Ephraim. In eternity, His bride will rule and reign with Him over all the nations of the earth.

Chapter 3
Ephraim—God's Firstborn

In Scripture, God calls Ephraim His firstborn: *"… for I am a Father to Israel, and Ephraim [Israel] is My firstborn" (Jeremiah 31:9, Amplified Bible).* According to the Law of Moses, all firstborns were set aside and consecrated to the Lord for His use—*"Sanctify (consecrate, set apart) to Me all the firstborn; whatever is first to open the womb among the Israelites, both of man and of beast, is Mine" (Exodus 13:2, Amplified Bible).* Upon the one designated firstborn, God bestowed special familial rights and responsibilities. As the leader of the family, the firstborn was also given a double portion (Deuteronomy 21:17).

God granted the right, authority, and responsibility to this family head to oversee the household's spiritual and financial trusts. That person was placed in the ruling position and expected to lead his brothers. It was considered a sacred, God-bestowed duty.

Attached to the right of the firstborn were significant blessings. But the birthright also came with the responsibility to follow God's commands, to carry out His purposes for the family, and in doing so, the earth and all mankind would be blessed. Above all, God would be glorified among the nations of the earth.

Therefore, as God's firstborn, the present-day descendants of Ephraim have the right, authority, and duty to take hold of the spiritual trust the Lord has bestowed upon them. (The financial trust is discussed in Part Two.) In the last hours of this present age, the responsibility has fallen to Ephraim to lead God's family in taking the gospel to the collapsing world.

Today, many of Ephraim's descendants are, indeed, leading family, friends, neighbors, and strangers into God's kingdom, and they are doing it with great fervor. Perhaps, just as many are not doing enough to build God's kingdom, and have busied themselves with the cares, burdens, and pleasures of the world. This is a grave mistake. God warned us that this present world-system is passing away. Christ is dismantling it, and everything we see today will, one day, be no more. The Lord is preparing an unprecedented, last days' move of His Spirit to usher millions into His kingdom before He closes out the age. His firstborn must be ready.

How Did Ephraim Become God's Firstborn?

Jacob, in his younger days, usurped the right of the firstborn from his elder brother, Esau, when he tricked his father Isaac, who was old and blind, into bestowing the birthright-blessing on him (Genesis 27). Afterward, Jacob had to flee the country. In exile, Jacob married two sisters, Leah and Rachel. Through these two and their two maidservants, Zilpah and Bilhah, Jacob produced 12 sons.

Reuben was Jacob's firstborn (through Leah), but he defiled his father's bed (Genesis 35:22, 49:3-4). Thus, on his deathbed,

Israel (formerly Jacob) gave the right of the firstborn to Joseph, his favorite son, who had been separated from his brothers for years in Egyptian bondage. He gave Joseph a double portion above his brothers: *"Moreover, I have given to you one portion above your brothers...." (Genesis 48:22).*

He also adopted Joseph's two sons as his own: *"And now your two sons, who were born to you in the land of Egypt before I came to you in Egypt, are mine; Ephraim and Manasseh shall be mine, as Reuben and Simeon are."* And *"May my name live on in them, and the names of my fathers, Abraham and Isaac" (Genesis 48:5, 16).* Thus, Joseph became two tribes through his sons, Manasseh and Ephraim.

Although Manasseh was the elder of Joseph's two sons, the right of the firstborn passed to Ephraim when Israel, in that same setting, crossed his arms and placed his right hand on Ephraim's head and his left hand on Manasseh's, and blessed them. By placing his right hand on Ephraim's head, Joseph's special birthright transferred to Ephraim.

Joseph sought to correct his father. He wanted the bequest to go to Manasseh, his true firstborn. Instead, Joseph was corrected by his father (Genesis 48:17-20).

In the eyes of the Lord, after the blessing had been bestowed, Ephraim now had the right to govern the family in spiritual and financial matters. He would lead the other 11 brothers. Whether that played out practically in real life during that time, only God knows. However, the ramifications of Israel's actions were sweeping, affecting future generations, including ours "for God's gifts and His call are irrevocable" (Romans 11:29).

The patriarch's blessing over Ephraim (and Manasseh) was significant in that it would set the course of nations. Israel prayed that both offspring would "grow into a multitude in the midst of the earth" (Genesis 48:16).

According to a commentary from Talmudic, Midrashic, and Rabbinic sources (The ArtsScroll Tanach Series) that meant: "May they proliferate abundantly like fish." Israel told Joseph that Manasseh would become a people, and his people would be great, but "the younger brother shall be greater than he, and his descendants shall become a *multitude* of nations" or *melo ha'goyim,* which in Hebrew meant "a fullness of Gentiles!" (Genesis 48:19).[1]

Over the past four millennia, Ephraim proliferated like fish, just as Israel prophesied. For more than two millennia, many of Ephraim's descendants have proclaimed Christ as their Lord and Savior. Today, Ephraim's progeny extends into a multitude of nations, fulfilling Israel's blessing over his favorite son's second child.

---

[1]Wootten, Batya, *Who is Israel? And Why You Should Know,* Key of David Publishing, 1984, p.17.

Chapter 4
Blinded Brothers Reunited

Both houses of Israel—Ephraim and Judah—have been blinded for many centuries. They will remain so until the "fullness of the Gentiles has come in" (Romans 11:25-26). Absorbed into the cultures of the world for thousands of years, Ephraim is more Gentile than Hebrew. Ephraim's descendants are completely unaware of their true lineage.

As a Gentile, Ephraim surely learned the ways of the Egyptians. (This is in view of the spiritual truth that the world is a place of bondage, a type of Egypt.) Ephraim thinks, walks, talks, and acts just like an Egyptian. In many ways, Ephraim is wedded to the world's systems, practices, and ways of doing things, but does not know many worldly customs and traditions are in direct conflict with the Torah. For these reasons, they are unrecognizable by those who live according to God's Law (Torah). Thus, Ephraim is to his Jewish brothers as Joseph was to his brothers—a Gentile, a stranger to God. But as we know from the story of Joseph, Joseph certainly knew God.

Joseph married the daughter of the Egyptian priest of On, Poti-Pherah. Pharaoh changed Joseph's name to Zaphnath-Paaneah.

By the time his brothers came looking for grain in Egypt during a time of great famine, Joseph had been completely absorbed into Egyptian culture. He looked, dressed, and spoke like an Egyptian. How could his brothers have recognized him? They didn't. They had no idea of their kinship to him.

Joseph's descendants have lived among Gentile cultures for thousands of years, and thus, their faith in, and love for, Christ has been intertwined with many aspects of pagan worship. But they do not know it. For example, the true origin of Christmas is pagan. Everything about Christmas—from the date of observance (December 25), to mistletoes, holly wreaths, Yule logs, the custom of exchanging gifts, even the Christmas tree—are rooted in pagan customs and practices!

Ephraim descendants demonstrate they have learned the ways of the nations when they cut down a Christmas tree and bring it into their homes during the Christmas holiday. The practice of bringing a felled tree into one's home and decorating it, finds its roots in the pagan cultures of ancient Egypt, Babylon, and Rome.

In ancient Babylonian culture, Nimrod was deified as the sun god. He was considered a branch of his mother. It was believed she mysteriously transformed into a tree before giving birth to him. Yule in Babylonian culture referred to an "infant" or "little child." Nimrod, who was cut down by his enemies, was brought back to life in the Yule log.

Thus, the practice of bringing a cut tree into the home represented a revival of the slain god, Nimrod! The tree—a palm tree in Egyptian culture and a fir tree in Roman culture—represented an idol. God's repeatedly warned His people not to bring idols into their homes (Deuteronomy 7:26, Jeremiah 10:2-4).

Likewise, the term Easter has nothing to do with the historical crucifixion and resurrection of Christ as many descendants of Ephraim believe. It, too, is Babylonian in origin. It is rooted in the celebration of the Chaldean goddess Astarte or Ishtar (Easter). The rabbit was her earthly symbol—a sign of fertility. This explains the presence of the Easter Bunny and Easter eggs. (Some believers who know better now simply refer to the sacred day of Christ's resurrection as Resurrection Sunday. Most Orthodox Christians refer to it as Pascha.)

Although plainly demonic, many in Ephraim ranks still celebrate Halloween. It is not recognized as the "hallowed eve" of All Saints' Day, November 1—a day set apart to commemorate all the saints martyred for the cause of Christ. Halloween is a day (or night) of revelry, to toast and give homage to the underworld. Many unsuspecting believers still blindly participate in the tribute.

Similarly, Ephraim does not know the pagan origins of her calendar—the days of the week (Monday through Sunday) or months of the year (January through December). The days of months on the Gregorian calendar are named after pagan deities.

Most sadly, many of Ephraim's descendants know nothing about the seven appointed Feasts (or Festivals) of the Lord. God commanded Israel to keep these as a "stature throughout all generations" (Leviticus 23). God bases His dealings with Israel and all the nations of the world upon these feasts. But Ephraim follows the Gregorian calendar and all its holidays. What are his modern Jewish brothers to think?

In fact, it is amazing how Satan has used Christians—many with Hebraic blood running through their veins—to persecute Jews down through the ages! Many of today's professing Christians are fiercely anti-Semitic. Christ says to those believers at this hour: "Wake up! I AM a Jew! So were My 12 disciples! There is no room for anti-Semitism or hatred of any kind in My Kingdom! Satan, the Father of Lies, has duped you!"

But they are not alone.

Judah, who loves the Torah, God's Law, has been blinded to the truth about her Messiah. More than 2,000 years after His First Advent, the Jews are *still* awaiting Messiah's arrival—not His return—His debut. God allowed this blindness because the proud, stiff-necked Jews of Christ's day missed the time of His visitation (Luke 19:41-44, 21:24). Judah, Christ says to you at this hour: "I AM the Messiah. There is no other Savior besides Me! Repent and be saved!"

Jews, as a people, missed Christ's First Coming. They did not realize their Messiah would first come like Joseph and later, like David. Christ came first as the Suffering-Servant Savior (Son of Joseph), but He shall return as a Conquering King (Son of David). As Messiah, He will rule the entire planet.

God will take the blinders off the two houses of Jacob, and bring them together during a time of horrific judgment. After that time of tribulation, when He has finished, a remnant of dispersed Jews and the scattered descendants of Ephraim will return, united, to the land God gave their forefathers, Abraham, Isaac, and Jacob.

Reunited After the Birth of a Special Child

Micah revealed the two lines will be reunited into one kingdom only *after* the *second* woman in Revelation 12 gives birth. Mary gave birth to Christ more than 2,000 years earlier. A second woman will give birth to another male child at the end of the age. (A fuller explanation of the second woman and second birth is given in Chapter 17.)

After the second woman gives birth to a male child, the Great Tribulation will begin. The second child's birth and snatching up will help usher in the Day of the Lord. Until the second woman gives birth, God will "give them up." That is, God will allow Ephraim and Judah to remain strangers to one another. The following journal excerpt reveals how the Lord first made this known to me.

February 28, 2012

> *Revisiting Micah 5:2-3*
>
> *Today, God has allowed me to see that the prophecy in Micah 5:2-3 is layered! Verses 2 and 3 pertain to the two women in Revelation 12, who bore children at two separate times more than 2,000 years apart. Micah 5:2 refers to Jesus Christ, who was born to Mary: "But, you, Bethlehem, Ephrathah, though you are little among the thousands of Judah, yet out of you shall come forth to Me the One to be Ruler in Israel, whose goings forth are from of old, from everlasting."*
>
> *Micah 5:3 refers to the second woman in Revelation 12:4 and 5b, who shall give birth to a son more than 2,000 years later, at the end of the age, just before Christ's Second Advent. At that time, Jesus Christ will reunite Judah (i.e., "remnant of His brethren") with Ephraim (i.e., "children of Israel"):*
>
> > *Therefore He shall give them up, until the time that she who is in labor has given birth; then the remnant of His brethren shall*

> *return to the children of Israel. And He [Christ] shall stand and feed his flock in the strength of the Lord, in the majesty of the name of the Lord His God; and they shall abide, for now He shall be great to the ends of the earth; and this One shall be peace (Micah 4:3-5).*

The Child Symbolizes Reunification

Why will Judah and Ephraim remain alienated until the second woman gives birth? One reason is the second child to whom the second woman gives birth, serves as a physical, living symbol of the reunification of the whole house of Israel. The Lord calls this second child Joshua, named for Himself. (Yeshua contracts to Joshua in Greek and English.)

December 19, 2004

Destiny's Child

Today, I heard God speak a special revelation to me through a sermon. The guest preacher brought a rich message about Moses being a child of destiny and Christ being the ultimate Destiny's Child because He delivered us from the bondage of sin and death. But as he spoke, I sensed the Lord talking to me about Joshua ... and myself.

About Joshua ...

A long time ago, the Lord convinced me the pattern of Moses' and Christ's births will repeat at the end of the age, at Joshua's birth. Joshua, the Lord's firstborn, will mark the end of an epoch and the beginning of a new one, just as the births of Moses and Christ did in their respective generations.

God raised up Moses to be a deliverer. Moses led God's people out of Egypt's bondage and brought them God's Law (Old Covenant). God raised up Christ to be the world's greatest Deliverer. He ushered in a New Covenant, saving mankind from the slavery of sin and death. Christ fulfilled all the requirements of the Law of Moses through His sacrifice on the cross.

Joshua's birth, like theirs, represents the end of some form of bondage or slavery and the dawning of a day of blessed deliverance. The Dragon, the Serpent of old (Satan), will try to devour Joshua at his birth just as he tried to destroy Moses and Christ at their births.

Joshua represents the unification of the 12 tribes of Israel after the Great Tribulation. He is the product of the Lion of Judah (Southern Kingdom) and a modern-day Samaritan woman (half Jew, half Gentile). She represents Ephraim (Northern Kingdom). The child is symbolic of the nation of Israel reunited in single person.

About Me ...

While my heart and mind were tuned to apply what I was hearing to Joshua, the Spirit kept reminding me that I was a child of destiny as well. For the first time, I felt God telling me I would be more than a "deliverer" of Joshua. I would also be a deliverer of His people. The message I will bring His people at the age's end will deliver many into His Kingdom.

The speaker made the following points about a destined child of God. They all struck my spirit with great force:

1. *God must join the two right persons to create a destined child, just as He did with Moses' parents, and later, with Mary, who was overshadowed by the Holy Spirit. (My parents were destined to give birth to me.)*
2. *Destiny is something one fulfills, accomplishes. It is not taught or learned. Moses was destined to be a deliverer of God's people before any of his days came to be. So was Christ. (So shall it be with me.)*
3. *Destiny is put into a person by God and guided by Him as the person lives. God's providence orchestrated both Moses' and Christ's life—from the womb to the tomb and beyond. (He is likewise guiding mine.)*
4. *God fully equips the destined child with everything the person needs to fulfill his or her destiny. God will not allow the deliverer's mission and purpose to be thwarted. Despite all, Moses and Christ accomplished their missions. (I shall accomplish mine.)*

5. *Destiny will always attract great opposition. Pharaoh and the protectors of Egypt's status quo feared and hated Moses. King Herod, the Sadducees, and Pharisees feared and hated Christ. (In my generation, leaders and status-quo keepers will fear and hate me.)*
6. *A destined child of God sometimes must be hidden from the world for a season. Moses was hidden in Pharaoh's court for 40 years and later, in the wilderness, for another 40 years. Christ was hidden as a child in Egypt to escape Herod and remained an obscure carpenter's Son until He was 30 years old. (I have been hidden for more than 51 years.)*
7. *The set and appointed time will come when the destined one cannot be hidden any longer. God called Moses out of the desert to confront Pharaoh. God called Christ out of Nazareth to confront sin and death. (I will be called to confront leaders who oppose God in my generation.)*
8. *Destiny is God's design. Man cannot control or manage it. It is guided by God's hand. God's Sovereign hand directed every aspect of Moses' life and that of Christ. Not one thing was ever out of God's control. (God alone is steering my destiny. I am not, nor is anyone else.)*
9. *There will be times when all must be entrusted to God. Moses' parents had to trust God would protect Moses in Pharaoh's house and court. Christ had to entrust His Father with His crucifixion. (At some point, I will be forced to entrust my life to God in a way I have never done before. Like Christ, I must set my face like a flint, and by His grace, weather what seems impossible.)*
10. *God will orchestrate many divine appointments on behalf of the destined one. Pharaoh's daughter was bathing in the Nile River when Moses floated to her in a basket. The shepherds and wise men were destined to find the Christ Child and honor Him. King Herod was not meant to find Him. (I have already experienced countless divine appointments. I don't think I will ever be able to recount them all.)*
11. *God will pour out His power and favor to help the destined individual fulfill his or her destiny. God gave Moses the power to smite Egypt with mighty plagues. Christ performed many miracles during His three and one half-year ministry to*

support His claim that He was God's Son. (Although I walk in God's authority, power, and favor now, I suspect these will be displayed in more spectacular ways as we draw closer to the Great Tribulation.)

Moses and Christ grew up to fulfill their destinies. After 430 years of bondage, Moses led the children of Israel out of Egyptian slavery to the Promised Land. Christ freed us from the bondage of sin and death. Soon He will return to remove His Church out of the world (Egypt) and deliver her to the ultimate Promised Land (Heaven). Her rapture will happen as God's judgment falls on the nations.

Afterward, Christ will return to earth to establish His millennial kingdom. At that time, He will reunite the 12 tribes of Israel. United, after more than 2,900 years of separation, Jacob's house will be a light unto the nations of the world. Israel's destiny will have been fulfilled.

Chapter 5

Idolatry Led to Loss of Hebrew Identity

Fifty years after God sent the Assyrians to conquer Israel's 10 tribes and sow them to the nations, the Assyrians sent foreigners from other conquered nations to help settle the northern territory of Ephraim. Overtime, the name Ephraim became synonymous with Israel and the Northern kingdom's capital city, Samaria.

The foreign settlers, who brought their gods with them, intermarried with the Israelite remnant left in the land. They created a mixed breed of people who were known as Samaritans in Christ's day (2 Kings 17:24-41, Ezra 4:2). The Samaritans were true descendants of Israel but mixed with Gentile blood. In the same vein, their worship of the Lord was not pure, but entangled in pagan practices and rituals. The Judeans loathed Samaritans (John 4:9). Among Judeans, Samaritans were considered a mongrel race. They were despised for their pagan religious practices and defiled bloodline.

But in all their righteousness (or lack of it), the Judeans missed the time of Christ's visitation! For their rejection of Christ as

Messiah, they were strewn to the nations in 70 A.D. when the Romans destroyed Jerusalem. A final dispersion occurred in 135 A.D. These Jews fled to Samaria, where their mixed brethren had settled centuries before them. And they journeyed to other lands beyond.

Consequently, the Northern Kingdom of Israel and the Southern Kingdom of Judah were effectively absorbed into the nations of the world to suffer the consequences of their unfaithfulness to God. The Lord promised they would pay if they ever disobeyed His commandments and refuse to repent.

Before the children of Israel entered the Promised Land of Canaan, God warned them through Moses that if they ever forsook His commandments and statutes, waves of dreadful curses would pursue and overtake them (Deuteronomy 28). He promised these plagues would devastate them and their progeny, ultimately returning their descendants to slavery. It would be a return to Egypt all over again!

Following is a sampling of the curses:

- Cursed shall you be in the city, and cursed shall you be in the country (v. 16).
- Cursed shall be your basket and your kneading bowl (v. 17).
- Cursed shall be the fruit of your body and the produce of your land, the increase of your cattle, and offspring of your flocks (v. 18).
- Cursed shall you be when you come in, and cursed shall you be when you go out (v. 19).
- The Lord will send on you cursing, confusion, and rebuke in all that you set your hand to do, until you are destroyed and until you perish quickly, because of the

wickedness of your doings in which you have forsaken Me (v. 20).

- The Lord will make the plague cling to you until He has consumed you from the land which you are going to possess (v. 21).
- The Lord will strike you with consumption, with fever, with inflammation, with severe burning fever, with the sword, with scorching and with mildew; they shall pursue you until you perish (v. 22).
- Your heavens which are over your head shall be bronze, and the earth which is under you shall be iron (v. 23).
- You shall betroth a wife, but another man shall lie with her, you shall build a house, but you shall not dwell in it, you shall plant a vineyard, but shall not gather its grapes (v. 30).
- Your sons and daughters shall be given to another people, and your eyes shall look and fail with longing for them all day long; and there shall be no strength in your hand (v. 32).
- You shall become an astonishment, a proverb, and a byword among the nations where the Lord will drive you (v. 37).
- A nation whom you have not known shall eat the fruit of your land and the produce of your labor, and you shall be only oppressed and crushed continually (v. 33).
- The alien who is among you shall rise higher and higher above you, and you shall come down lower and lower (v. 43).
- He shall lend to you, but you shall not lend to him; he shall be the head and you shall be the tail (v. 44).
- Moreover, all these curses shall come upon you and pursue and overtake you, until you are destroyed because you did not obey the voice of the Lord your God, to keep His commandments and His statutes which He commanded you. And they shall be upon you for a sign

and a wonder, and on your descendants forever (vv. 45-46).

- Therefore, you shall serve your enemies, whom the Lord will send against you, in hunger, in thirst, in nakedness, and in need of everything; and He will put a yoke of iron on your neck until He has destroyed you (v. 48).
- The Lord will bring a nation against you from afar, from the end of the earth, as swift as the eagle flies, a nation whose language you will not understand, a nation of fierce countenance, which does not respect the elderly nor show favor to the young (v. 49-50).
- Then the Lord will scatter you among all peoples, from one end of the earth to the other, and there you shall serve other gods, which neither you nor your fathers have known—wood and stone (v. 65).
- And among those nations you shall find no rest, nor shall the sole of your foot have a resting place; but there the Lord will give you a trembling heart, failing eyes, and anguish of soul (v. 66)
- Your life will hang in doubt before you; you shall fear day and night and have no assurance of life. In the morning, you shall say, "Oh, that it were evening!" And at evening you shall say, "Oh, that it were morning!" because of the fear which terrifies your heart, and because of the sight which your eyes see (v. 67).

God promised the curses would render them small in number as a people: *"You shall be left, few in number, whereas you were as the stars of heaven in multitude, because you would not obey the voice of the Lord your God"* (v. 62).

But there was more.

In the last verse of Deuteronomy 28, God promised He would ultimately send them off to slavery in slave ships! *"And the Lord will take you back to Egypt in ships, by the way of which I said to you, 'You shall never see again.' And there you shall be offered for sale to your enemies as male and female slaves...."* (v. 68).

Surely, the descendants of Israel suffered the curses of Deuteronomy 28 when they were conquered by the Assyrians in 722 B.C. and by the Babylonians in 586 B.C. However, in neither case was it necessary for them to be put on ships since Assyria and Babylon share the same land mass as Israel! Further, the Judeans dispersed by Rome in 70 A.D., throughout the Middle East, Africa, Europe, and nations beyond, were never taken on slave ships.

So, when were the Israelite rebels taken on slave ships?

Many of Jacob's descendants were taken on ships during the Transatlantic Slave Trade! That is when this ancient prophecy was fulfilled! The Transatlantic Slave Trade began in the fifteenth century and lasted more than four centuries.

In a migration that would take roughly 1,200 years, an untold number of scattered Judeans migrated south from Jerusalem through Egypt and Ethiopia, across the sub-Saharan Africa, to the West Coast of Africa, where they eventually built three great *pagan* empires—Ghana, Mali, and Songhai. Let us remember, these refugees were primarily the descendants of two tribes—Judah and Benjamin.[2] The other tribes had been disseminated into the nations nearly eight centuries earlier, and undoubtedly had descendants throughout the world by the time the Judeans were scattered.

---

[2]*During the time of Israel's split into two kingdoms, the priests, Levites, and other members of Israel's Northern tribes defected to the Southern Kingdom of Judah, under Solomon's son, Rehoboam (2 Chronicles 11:13-17).*

The last of the great African empires, Songhai (670 to 1591 A.D.), was decimated by the slave trade. Because of their unrelenting idolatry, these Jewish migrants were put on slave ships to the New World, taken to the Western Hemisphere—South America, Central America, North America, and the West Indies. In these new lands, they lost their Hebrew identity. But through centuries of brutal slavery, oppression, and hardship, many came to embrace Jesus Christ as their Lord and Savior.

Chapter 6
Restoration of Hebrew Identity

In Revelation 7:1-8, God seals a missionary corps of 144,000 zealots to do His bidding during the Great Tribulation. All 144,000 are from the House of Israel. They are identified by their 12 tribes with 12,000 members in each tribe. They are a kind of "firstfruits" of a fuller restoration of Israel under Christ's millennial reign (Revelation 14:14).

For the Lord to seal His servants, their Hebraic heritage and identities must be restored. Many Old Testament prophets foretold of Israel's restoration:

- *Arise, shine; for your light has come! And the glory of the Lord is risen upon you. For behold, the darkness shall cover the earth, and deep darkness the people; but the Lord will arise over you, and His glory will be seen upon you. The Gentiles shall come to your light, and kings to the brightness of your rising (Isaiah 60:1-3).*

- *For I will take you from among the nations, gather you out of all the countries, and bring you into your own land. Then, I will sprinkle clean water on you, and you shall be clean; I will cleanse you from all your filthiness and from all your idols. I will give you a new heart and put a new spirit within you ... I will put My Spirit within you and cause you to walk in My statutes, and you will keep My judgments and do them (Ezekiel 36:24-27).*

- *I will heal their backsliding. I will love them freely, for My anger has turned away from him. I will be like the dew to Israel; He shall grow like the lily and lengthen his roots like Lebanon. His branches shall spread; His beauty shall be like an olive tree and his fragrance like Lebanon ... Ephraim will say, "What have I to do anymore with idols?" (Hosea 14:4-6, 8).*

- *"The Redeemer will come to Zion, and to those who turn from transgression in Jacob," says the Lord. "As for Me," says the Lord, "this is My Covenant with them: My Spirit who is upon you, and My words which I have put in your mouth, shall not depart from your mouth, nor from the mouth of your descendants, nor from the mouth of your descendants' descendants," says the Lord, "from this time and forevermore" (Isaiah 59:20-21).*

- *And I will cause the captives of Judah and the captives of Israel to return and will rebuild those places as at the first. I will cleanse them from their iniquity by which they have sinned against Me, and I will pardon all their iniquities by which they have sinned and by which they have transgressed Me. Then it shall be to Me a name of joy, a praise and an honor before all the nations of the earth, who shall hear all the good that I do to them; they shall fear and tremble for all the goodness and all the prosperity that I provide it (Jeremiah 33:7-9).*

We are fast approaching the season when Christ will reveal the identity of Israel's descendants to themselves and to the world. Their millennia-long trek across lands of the earth has rendered Israel's seed a mixed multitude in the earth, just as God promised the Patriarchs they would be! As a "multitude of the Gentiles", they could be called modern-day Samaritans—half

Hebrew, half Gentile! From among them shall arise a subset of Jacob's seed—the Josephs—whom God will greatly use for His end-time purposes.

The Rise of the Josephs

Just as God raised up Joseph during a period of unparalleled famine in Egypt, He will raise up a segment of modern-day "Samaritans"—the Josephs—during the Great Tribulation. They are born-again descendants of the tribe of Ephraim. During a last days' monumental crisis, God will use them mightily for His glory. A spiritual famine of unprecedented proportions will have overtaken the world. These sold-out believers will aggressively and uninhibitedly proclaim Christ's salvation truth to a world crumbling under a surging tide of extraordinary wickedness.

At this time, the Josephs will help unite the body of Christ across racial, denominational, and national lines. This great army of mighty witnesses will galvanize her members to act as "one man" with "one mind" and "one heart" for "one purpose"— the salvation of souls. God will use the Josephs to "save many people alive" during the great famine of our generation.

God's contemporary Josephs will be to the world what Joseph was to the world in his generation—a type of savior, a deliver. God will use them to usher in a spiritual revival, the likes the world has never seen. After that period, He will rapture His bride out of the world and pour His full wrath on the nations.

Chapter 7
Reemergence and Preeminence of Joseph as a Tribe

Scripture indicates during the Day of the Lord there shall reemerge a single tribe under the banner of Joseph within the 12 tribes of Israel. The tribe of Joseph will assume a special leadership role within the family of God. On Israel's deathbed, the patriarch blessed his 12 sons. But Joseph, who had been separated from his brothers in Egypt and who rose to become second to Pharaoh, received the longest and most exceptional blessing. Israel's blessing served almost as a consecration on Joseph's life. It forecasted what would become of him and his descendants:

> *Joseph is a fruitful bough, a fruitful bough by a well; his branches run over the wall. The archers have bitterly grieved him, shot at him and hated him. But his bow remained in strength, and the arms of his hands were made strong by the hand of the Mighty God of Jacob (From there is the Shepherd, the Stone of Israel), by the God of your father who will help you, and by the Almighty who will bless you with blessings of heaven above, blessings of the deep that lies beneath, blessings of the breasts and of the womb. The blessings of your father have excelled the blessings of my ancestors, up to the utmost bound of the everlasting hills. They*

shall be on the head of him who was separate from his brothers (Genesis 49:22-26).

As discussed earlier, Israel adopted Joseph's sons, Ephraim and Manasseh, as his own. Israel passed the right of the firstborn from Reuben (eldest) to Joseph, and from Joseph to Ephraim. Four hundred and thirty years later, Moses numbered Joseph's sons, Ephraim and Manasseh, among Israel's 12 tribes. The two had rightly replaced their father Joseph, per Israel's last wishes (Numbers 1:20-43).

However, in the day of God's final judgment on the nations, Manasseh is still listed among the 12 tribes, but Ephraim is not. Instead, Joseph reappears as one of the 12 tribes. Joseph replaces Ephraim (Revelation 7:5-8) apparently in preparation for God's veiled, end-time purposes.

Thus, 12,000 descendants of the tribe of Joseph shall be raised up along with 12,000 descendants of the tribe of Manasseh, as part of God's mighty army of 144,000 Hebrew witnesses during the Great Tribulation (Revelation 7:6, 8). The tribe of Joseph will lead the tribes in this matchless spiritual crusade.

As an aside, Dan is omitted from the final list of tribes in Revelation 7:5-8. Some Biblicists believe Dan's absence may trace to its role in leading Israel into idolatry (1 Kings 12:28-30, 2 Kings 10:29) or the abandonment of its land allotment in Joshua's day (Joshua 19:40-48) to migrate to the extreme north of Israel (Judges 18:1-31). It seems Dan's fate fulfills his father's last words to him: *"Dan shall be a serpent by the way, a viper in the path that bites the horse's heels so that its rider shall fall backward"* (Genesis 49:17).

The Prophet Ezekiel may shed further light on the reemergence of Joseph as a tribe in the latter days. A careful study of Ezekiel 37 shows Joseph will play a lead role in the reunification of the 12 tribes. God will reunite the 12 tribes under Christ's headship. This is aptly symbolized by the two sticks God commanded Ezekiel to unite.

The Lord commanded Ezekiel to take *"the stick of Joseph, which is in the hand of Ephraim and the tribes of Israel, his companions"* and join them to Judah to make one stick. In other words, Ephraim (as a single tribe) holds the stick that represents Joseph. That same stick also represents *"all the rest of Israel, his companions"* (i.e., Northern tribes). It will be joined to Judah's stick, and they shall become one in God's hand:

- *As for you, son of man, take a stick for yourself and write on it: "For Judah and for the children of Israel, his companions." Then take another stick and write on it, "For Joseph, the stick of Ephraim, and for all the house of Israel, his companions." Then join them one to another for yourself into one stick, and they shall become one in your hand (Ezekiel 37:15-17).*

- *Thus, says the Lord God: "Surely I will take the stick of Joseph which is in the hand of Ephraim, and the tribes of Israel, his companions: and I will join them with it, with the stick of Judah, and make them one stick, and they will be one in My hand" (Ezekiel 37:19).*

- *Surely, I will take the children of Israel from among the nations, wherever they have gone, and will gather them from every side and bring them into their own land; and I will make them one nation in the land, on the mountains of Israel; and one king shall be king over them all; they shall no longer be two nations, nor shall they ever be divided into two kingdoms again (Ezekiel 37:21-22).*

Who are God's Latter-Day Josephs?

For sure, only God knows who His modern-day Josephs are. They are the descendants of the tribe of Ephraim *before* the entire Northern Kingdom of Israel became synonymous with, and known as, Ephraim. Does Scripture offer any clues about who the Josephs might be? Absolutely!

The Mark of "the Josephs"

What are the markers identifying a person as "a Joseph?" And once, identified, what is a member of this tribe expected to do? We can examine the life of the Joseph, the prototype, to garner clues on who might have membership in this powerful army of final-hour evangelists and what God will require of them.

The Mark—

1. A people descendant from the house of Israel (Jacob).
2. A people of both Semitic and Hamitic heritage as Joseph (Semitic) and wife, Asenath (Hamitic), bore Manasseh and Ephraim, who were both Semitic and Hamitic.
3. A people whose feet were put in fetters, sold into slavery by their brothers, as was Joseph.
4. A people torn from their homeland and sent off to a foreign land to live among people whom they did not know, who spoke a language they did not understand, and whose customs and conventions were different from their own, as was Joseph's experience.
5. A people residing mostly in bountiful nations, as Joseph resided in Egypt, known then as the "breadbasket of the world."
6. A people of many hues and colors, as symbolized by Joseph's coat.

7. A people in whom God developed a deep compassion for the poor, disenfranchised, and marginalized, "as if chained with them," as was Joseph's case.
8. A people who are a byword, a reproach, a proverb in their host lands, as was Joseph.
9. A people considered dispensable by many, but seen as a peculiar treasure to God, as was Joseph.
10. A people beleaguered by many inequities and injustices in their host lands, yet they persevere through them, as did Joseph.
11. A people who have been severely pruned ("cut back") multiple times, as was Joseph, to bear much fruit for God, as did Joseph.
12. A people walking in God's hidden, uncommon favor, as did Joseph.
13. A people whose ancestors built their masters' estates and nations, as Joseph built Potiphar's estate and Joseph's seed built Egypt.
14. A people visited by God with interpretable visions and dreams that come to past, as did Joseph's dreams.
15. A people envied by their brothers for their visions and dreams, as was Joseph.
16. A people whose work slowly prospered from God's favor, despite inordinate obstacles and setbacks, as Joseph's work prospered in God's hand.
17. A people who walk in the teaching and instruction of God's Word and have been tested and proven by it, as was Joseph.
18. A people who have been trained and honed through affliction, and are no longer self-focused, pampered, or spiritually immature, mirroring the way God prepared and matured Joseph.
19. A people, unrecognizable by their Jewish brethren, because of their "Egyptian" trappings, just as Joseph was unrecognizable by his brothers.

20. A people whose ancestors were slaves for roughly four centuries, as Joseph's ancestors were enslaved for four centuries after his death.
21. A people presently hidden in the pits of life, who will rise meteorically out of nowhere to assume their divinely appointed roles in the same way Joseph rose from a prison felon to ruler.
22. A people who will rise to a place of prominence by way of a large-scale crisis; they will be respected for their gifts and talents in their host lands, as Joseph was revered by his Egyptian hosts in the end.

The Assignment—

1. A people who are Spirit-filled, Spirit-controlled, Spirit-led, who, by experience, know nothing is impossible for God, just as Joseph discovered after years of unjust suffering.
2. A people who faced many hardships, stretched beyond their human limits and pulverized into "a balm of Gilead," as was Joseph. God crushed them to bring relief and healing to others, as He did Joseph.
3. A people who will have doors divinely opened for them to help the suffering after enduring much affliction, just as Joseph endured and God opened doors for him.
4. A people who will be raised up at a set and appointed time to solve an epic crisis allowed by God, as Joseph was raised up during Egypt's great famine.
5. A people who will be given a significant spiritual and financial trust to manage for God's glory, as prophesied by Israel (Jacob) and Moses.
6. A people who will be commanding witnesses for God in a time of widespread desolation, as was Joseph during Egypt's famine.
7. A people walking in God's wisdom, who will instruct others on how to survive in a time of unprecedented

want, as did Joseph.

8. A people who will control and oversee God's spiritual and physical storehouses during the time of great famine as did Joseph.
9. A people destined to bring blessings to their brethren, whose kindred sold their ancestors into slavery, just as Joseph was a blessing to his brethren and their progeny, many years after he was sold into slavery.
10. A people who will throw off their "Egyptian" garments when they realize who they are, just as Joseph requested that even his bones, one day, be carried out of Egypt and taken to the Promised Land.
11. A people who will plunder "Egypt", just as the children of Israel (Joseph and his brothers' descendants) plundered Egypt before they left.
12. A people who will forgive great trespasses, just as Joseph forgave his brothers' great trespasses and Egypt's ill-treatment and abuse of him.

What Joseph was forced to endure as a slave in Egypt sounds eerily like the experience of many of today's African American and West Indian believers, who overcame a bitter slavery past to embrace Christ as their Messiah! During the Transatlantic Slave Trade, Africans were sold into slavery by their brothers for profit and to halt tribal rivalries. The Transatlantic Slave Trade began in the 1440s, and ended in the United States, in 1865. Consequently, these transplants endured more than 400 years of cruel enslavement. Slavery's abolishment in the U.S. has still been followed by more than 150 years of institutional or systemic racism. God's plan is to use a titanic evil for great good, as He did with Joseph.

The Josephs Destined to "Save Many People Alive"

There is a fish native to Japan that grows only two to three inches in size if kept in a fishbowl. But that fish can grow a foot if put in a pond. It can grow more than three feet long if put out to sea. This fish aptly describes Joseph and his modern-day descendants!

Joseph was too much fish for his tank! God had to transport the original prototype to a "bigger pond" to manifest the blessing He commanded on Abraham's ancestry (Genesis 12:2-3). Joseph needed a sea for God to expose the potential and gifts He put inside him! So, God moved Joseph from the tribal community of his birth to the booming empire of Egypt. Only in Egypt could the decreed blessing on Abraham's line that was on Joseph's life, be revealed to the world.

Joseph was an Old Testament type and shadow of a truth under the New Covenant of Christ. God will raise up a specially-prepared people to feed and nurture the masses—and save Israel's heritage—at the age's close for His glory. They will be powerful witnesses to God's goodness and greatness to a spiritually and physically famished world.

As it went with Joseph, so shall it be with Joseph's descendants. They *had* to be transported to a land of captivity, to an Egypt, for God to develop and grow them—across the centuries—for a set and designated time on His calendar. Our Lord saw the great end-time famine coming "far off" and He prepared.

Chapter 8
The Josephs—A Hidden Stradivarius

While others saw a lowly Hebrew slave, a foreign outcast, a convicted felon in Joseph, God perceived a consummate administrator. The Lord saw the next Prime Minister of Egypt. Sitting in an Egyptian jail cell, Joseph had not the slightest clue that God would raise him up to be the second highest-ranking officer in Egypt.

Likewise, many of us modern-day Josephs have not the tiniest inkling of the great and breathtaking plan God has in store for us. We so frequently feel overwhelmed and defeated by our circumstances and setbacks. We are often made to feel less than, inferior to others. But God showed me one day in late 1998 that He does not view us—His special workmanship in progress—the same way others perceive us or even in the same way we see ourselves.

The day was Sunday, November 1, 1998. Sitting alone on the end of a church pew, I felt lower than the floor. I had been struggling with depression for two days. My problems seemed like huge walls before me. I would claw my way to a mountain summit, only to find a whole range of crags and cliffs to next traverse. The grueling, arduous journey appeared endless. I was worn out by the clawing, scraping, and climbing. For days, weeks, months, I felt a creeping hopelessness and despair weighing me down. Now it had overtaken me.

I could not seem to make a dent in anything. I was keenly aware of the enemy's scheme to oppose anything I tried. One step forward, two steps backward. Three steps forward, five steps backward. I felt blocked, hindered, thwarted on all sides. God gave me several dreams, confirming what I felt. The enemy sought to restrict or confound my every move. *When will I come out of this pit? Lord, when will you say, "Enough!"* As I struggled with these feelings, a guest pastor at our church took the podium. He began to tell a story.

The pastor explained to the congregation that someone in his family was engaged to an accomplished violinist. One night, over dinner, the bride to be shared with the other dinner guests the most recent counsel her instructor had given her. Her music would never improve beyond where she was until she invested in a new violin. The new violin would cost $20,000 and the bow, another $10,000.

Upon hearing this, the congregation gasped. At that point, the pastor informed us there were violins that cost $250,000. This led to a discussion about the most valuable violins in the world, those made by Antonio Stradivari. These violins can cost millions of dollars. Many of them are now in fine museums throughout the world.

"Can you really tell the difference between a Stradivari violin and other violins?" the family questioned. The woman assured them that she could and explained why.

Antonio Stradivari was an impoverished violin maker. He could not afford the fine wood that other violin makers used. He pulled his wood from polluted, wind-swept docks and moors on the edges of the city. He cleaned it up and dried it out. Then, he carved and chiseled the battered, weathered wood into extraordinary, fine instruments of music.

Experts have examined his violins to learn what gives them their incomparable sound. They discovered the cells of the wood were hollowed and eaten away from the mud, debris, and polluted water. But after being cleaned, dried, and fashioned into a vessel of music, that weather-beaten instrument became unsurpassed in creating melodious sounds. The melody fills the hollow cells, making a solitary violin resonate with the extraordinary sound of a multitude of violins!

Violins made by Stradivari more than 250 years ago, have never been surpassed in tone, power, and form. This makes them incomparable, priceless, coveted treasures. According to the World Book Encyclopedia, "Stradivari violins have become the unrivaled ideals of tonal perfection and beauty of workmanship. Stradivari is considered the greatest violin maker of all time."

Sitting there listening to all this, a thought struck me with great force. I nearly jumped out of my seat. I had to contain myself, to keep from shouting: "I'm a Stradivarius!"

Is this not exactly what Christ did for me? I thought. He pulled me out of the muck and mire of the tragic choices of my life. He rescued me from my sin and that of others, which had left me empty and hollow inside. He found me on the edges of life, in the margins, on the trash heap. Undaunted by my wounds and stench, He cleaned me up and dried me out. Afterward, He filled me with Himself.

Next, He began conforming me—no chiseling me—into a magnificent instrument. His seemingly endless sculpting was the source of my pain! My God was transforming me, so that one day, whenever I performed or acted on His behalf, I would be a melodious symphony to Him. My life would be a beautiful concerto to my Creator, incomparable in tone, power, and form!

The instant this truth gripped my soul, my spirit soared. My depression vanished. Seeing God's hand in my suffering this way, yanked me out of my despondency and catapulted me to the heights!

Josephs, we are one of a kind! As we give ourselves away—pour our talents, gifts, lives into others against all odds and obstacles—God takes immense pleasure in us. Sacrificially spending ourselves to serve and refresh others delights Him. We are the Master's workmanship, chips off the Old Block—pieces of the Master, in fact, Masterpieces!

We are priceless treasures to Him, a peculiar people in the earth, and He has freed and blessed us in every way, to become who He has called us to be. We have been fashioned for His blessed, divine purposes. He filled us with Himself to accomplish good and mighty works in His name during our lifetimes, despite what has been done to us. He is using every obstruction, every hindrance, and every injustice to mold and make us usable for His glorious purposes. We must *always* remember Joseph was the blessed one.

Joseph—The Blessed One

I will never forget how the Lord first introduced the truth to me that Joseph was, indeed, the blessed one, irrespective of circumstances. It was on a cold night in February 2000. I was invited by my friends, Jerome and Alena Edmondson, to attend a gala event at the Cobo Hall Arena in downtown Detroit. I attended along with 400 other African American professionals.

Much to everyone's surprise, at the beginning of the night's event, an African king took the stage. He apologized to the audience on behalf of *his* ancestors for selling *our* ancestors into slavery. At the end of his brief message, he reminded us all that, as was in the case of Joseph, history will prove we were the blessed ones.

Days after the king's apology, the Lord began to show me astounding parallels between African Americans and Joseph. Afterward, He gave me a coat of many colors, started calling me Joseph and sent me around the country to speak to African American audiences. I told them how, one day, God would resurrect them out of their pits to serve Him during a time of great famine. The following introduction to a speech, given at a United Negro College Fund fundraiser, recapitulates the king's apology:

March 17, 2000

"You Can Call Me Jo(seph)!"

Last month, I had the pleasure of meeting the King of Togo, his Majesty King F.A. Ayi. He is the symbolic king of his country, much like Queen Elizabeth is the symbolic queen of England. Togo is a small nation on the West Coast of Africa, right in the heart of what used to be called the Slave Coast. As many of you know, most

African Americans are descendants of the African tribes, located on or near the West Coast of Africa.

In a setting, much like this one, the king addressed an audience of 400 African Americans. Tall and regal, he approached the podium in all his African regalia. His address took us all by surprise.

A Christian king of not more than 35 years of age, he quietly and humbly took the microphone. In his beautiful, accented English, the king proceeded to ask the audience for forgiveness. I remember clearly his words: "As an African chief, and on behalf of all the African chiefs, past and present, I ask that you forgive us for selling you, our brothers, into slavery."

You could hear a pin drop. The audience was motionless. We were stunned and awed by his humility. He shared how he had come under criticism by some in his country, and in other parts of Africa, for apologizing for his ancestors' participation in the slave trade. Some believed it beneath a king to ask for forgiveness. But he felt God had called him to convey this sentiment to African Americans, whenever and wherever he spoke in the States.

We were all deeply moved. No one had ever expressed regret for the injustices of our slave past. The king closed his message with this statement: "Remember, Joseph was the blessed one."

The king's point was a salient, powerful one. God used Joseph's suffering to bless Israel's heritage, Egypt, and others, beyond anything Joseph could have ever imagined. Again, Joseph's life serves as an Old Testament type and shadow of a truth that will repeat under the New Covenant. In the latter days, God will use the suffering of Joseph's progeny to bless Israel and the entire world ("Egypt").

Chapter 9
God's Army of Josephs!

On July 14, 2003, the Lord gave me a dream, in which I saw thousands of black fish assemble like an army in the ocean. At first there were scores, then there were hundreds, and then there were thousands. I was on the ship, looking out at the ocean in awe. All I could see for miles and miles were black fish, lining up, one row behind another, standing at attention, looking up at the ship. The dream ended with fish still coming.

The fish symbolized a spiritual army of Josephs that the Lord Himself will assemble at a set time near the close of the age. They are the tribe of Joseph, progeny of Joseph's youngest son, Ephraim, who was given the right of the firstborn by Israel (Jacob): *"... I will lead them back; I will cause them to walk by streams of water and bring them in a straight way in which they will not stumble, for I am a Father to Israel, and Ephraim is My firstborn" (Jeremiah 31:9).*

The fish in my dream were black because of their Hamitic roots. They are the descendants of former African slaves, who were taken from the Motherland of Africa and brought to the

Americas during the Transatlantic Slave Trade that lasted more than four centuries. They are true Israelites!

Black is also the color of death. These fish have died to self. They have gone to their funerals. They have died to the world and its frills. The world's trappings of wealth, power, fame, and the pursuit of self-actualization and self-achievement have lost their allure. Satan's spell has been broken off their minds. Their hearts are no longer shackled to temporal things. They are FREE!

They now understand *everything* the eye can see will soon be no more. But a human soul, which the eye cannot see, will live forever. A soul will either live in the presence of its Almighty Creator for all eternity. Or, it will dwell in hell where there is "wailing and gnashing of teeth" and "the worm never dies and the fire is never quenched" (Luke 13:28, Mark 44, 48).

Hell's inhabitants are removed from God's presence forever. There is no house big enough, no car fast enough, no career prestigious enough, no fame wide enough, and no person handsome, gorgeous, lovely, charming, or winsome enough to exchange for that eternal fate.

The Josephs have a pivotal role to play in the new season the Church is about to enter. It is the Feast of Trumpets Season.

The Feast of Trumpets Season

Beloved of the Lord, we have entered the last chapter of God's Redemption Story—a love story, spanning six millennia. Christ will soon, physically, return to earth. A new epoch is about to begin. The Feast of Trumpets Season will kick start the new Messianic age.

In modern times, Feast of Trumpets marks the beginning of Israel's New Year (Rosh Hashanah). It signifies a time of God calling His people together, in solemn assembly, to repent in preparation for His judgment. Many people are unaware that Feast of Trumpets, as with all of God's feasts, signifies so much more.

Feast of Trumpets is a time of the blowing of the trumpets (or Shofar). In ancient times, the blowing of the Shofar warned God's people that war was imminent. It also signaled a bridegroom coming unexpectedly for his waiting bride.

God ordained seven feasts (or festivals) for the ancient Hebrews as lasting statutes to be practiced *forever* throughout their generations. Each of these appointed feasts is a holy convocation or sacred assembly. God ordained these seven feasts as rehearsals or recitals for His great plan to reveal the Messiah's First and Second Comings (Colossians 2:16-17).

The Prophet Hosea prophesied that the Messiah's First and Second Advents will be like the "former and latter rains" (Hosea 6:3). The former rain refers to the four spring feasts, and the latter rain refers to three fall feasts. Christ's two appearances tie to these Hebraic festivals.

The first four feasts (or festivals) pointed to Christ's First Coming as the Suffering-Servant Savior. The Feast of Passover signified His death. The Feast of Unleavened Bread denoted His burial. The Feast of Firstfruits stood for His resurrection. Pentecost symbolized the giving of the Holy Spirit.

The last three festivals—Feast of Trumpets (Rosh Hashanah), Day of Atonement (Yom Kippur) and Feast of Tabernacles

(Sukkot) point to Christ's Second Coming as the Triumphant Conquering Messiah.

During Feast of Trumpets, the Bridegroom will call His bride out of the world before He judges it. Day of Atonement points to a day of worldwide repentance after Christ is revealed to all as the True Messiah. Feast of Tabernacles looks forward to the time when Immanuel ("God with us") will "tabernacle" (i.e., live) with His people on earth in Jerusalem.

Chapter 10
The Josephs' Role in the Feast of Trumpets Season

Scripture teaches Feast of Trumpets began with Joseph (not Moses) as a testimony when he "went out over the land." When did Joseph go out over the land? We are told twice in Genesis that Joseph went out over the land of Egypt after being appointed Prime Minister by Pharaoh before the great famine (Genesis 41:45-46).

What possibly could have been Joseph's purpose for this? What was his testimony? Joseph, an Israelite, and by this time, a staunch believer in the Yahweh Elohim, no doubt warned the people of God's plan to send a ruinous famine. The famine, covering the entire planet, would do the unthinkable—ravish Egypt, the most prosperous nation on earth. Surely, Joseph warned the people to prepare and initiated his solemn message by the blowing of the trumpets as an alarm.

This is yet another Old Covenant picture of a New Covenant reality. The time is upon us when God's modern-day Josephs must "sound the alarm" for the peoples of the world ("Egypt") to prepare spiritually for another "famine" that will ravish the nations.

The famine of our time is the Great Tribulation. During this period, people will find themselves in terrible physical want, in need of food. They will also be in great spiritual want, in need of spiritual bread—The Living Bread—Christ. The Josephs will lead the body of Christ in bringing physical and spiritual manna to the ravenous masses.

The Holy Spirit will revive Israel's "old dry bones" just as God promised. His Josephs will help the resurrected, revived, and called-out descendants of Israel's ancient tribes to lead the body of Christ in a worldwide revival. At the eleventh hour of our present age, Christ's army of Josephs will ignite a global evangelical movement the world has never experienced. No corner of the earth will remain untouched. During this consummate move of the Spirit, millions of souls will be guided into God's kingdom.

God will assemble these fishers of men to help open the eyes of those whose names are written in the Lamb's Book of Life, but who have not yet entered the Good Shepherd's sheep pen. They will say to those who have already entered, "Wake up! Join us!"

Our Lord shall not lose one of His chosen. Not one whom the Father has placed in the Son's hand will He cast out. There is no pit too deep or so dark that He cannot pull out with a Strong Arm and Mighty Hand.

The set and appointed time approaches. As God prepares to close out this age, He will call His Josephs from their pits, where

He has hidden them. They will be spectacular witnesses for Christ. In the secret places where He primed them, they have come to know Him quite intimately. They rejoice over Him and trust in His goodness, power, and blood. He hears their cries and petitions and answers them.

> *... I will save the house of Joseph. I will bring them back, because I have mercy on them. They shall be as though I had not cast them aside; for I am the Lord their God, and I will hear them. Those of Ephraim shall be like a mighty man, and their hearts shall rejoice as if with wine ... I will whistle for them and gather them, for I will redeem them and they shall increase as they once increased (Zechariah 10:6-8).*

Joseph, you are not cast off. God has not forgotten you. In the pit, where you are right now, ponder these 12 truths. Recite them to yourselves. Allow them to fortify your soul:

1. My life is not my own. I have no claims to it. What else do I have to do with my life that is better than what God has planned?
2. I did not create myself, so I do not know what is best for me.
3. I have all eternity to live. I need not try to escape the pit. I must be ready, prepared, trained to master what is coming.
4. I have glimpsed the Prize. He is well worth waiting for. (What did I expect, if I am to obtain such a Prize?)
5. There is nothing behind me. Do not bother to look back. Standing still is not an option. I must go onward and upward.

6. I do not know what is around the next corner since I am not the Author of my story. God is. I will fret nothing, nor will I jump ahead of Him.
7. I am in the forefront of an unfolding cosmic war-adventure. I have a duty to accept it, embrace it. I will not retreat from it or try to escape it.
8. Good things will happen as well as the "not so good." God uses both for my everlasting benefit.
9. I am in the "making place" (i.e., world's womb) being made ready for my eternal role on the other side of this bedlam. I must not squander my small window of opportunity.
10. Let God pace me. Just do each day what He puts before me, trusting Him, and I will arrive at my destined end.
11. The only way forward is to die to self and stay dead. Endure for the sake of the Prize set before me.
12. Sacrificial love is the only way out.

At this hour, the Lord of Hosts and our Commander and Chief says:

> "Get ready, Joseph! Your time has come! This is your season! This is your hour! You have been trained and raised up for such a time as this. You have been divinely prepared and strategically placed! Take up your position of faith, and await your Master's instructions. A 'famine' is coming to ravish the land—a physical and spiritual deprivation the earth has never seen. You will be released to perform great exploits during this time. By My Mighty Hand, I will use you to 'save many people alive' in the last hours of the age!"

PART TWO:
Ephraim's Hidden Treasure

Chapter 11
A Blessing from Beneath: Crude Oil!

"... the Almighty, who will bless you with blessings of heaven above, blessings of the deep that lies beneath...." (Genesis 49:25).

"... Blessed of the Lord is his land, with the precious things of heaven, with the dew, and the deep lying beneath...." (Deuteronomy 33:13).

I was called to Hawaii on business. Or, so I thought at the time. The trip occurred right around the time God began to unveil the mystery of Israel's 10 tribes to me. I arrived in Hawaii on August 20, 2002 just in time to give my speech. Everything went well with the speech that took only an hour. I could not help but wonder why the Lord had me travel such a great distance for such a small cause. As it turned out, the speech was just a ploy to get me to Hawaii. More importantly, God wanted to nail a point.

In time, I became convinced that 2002 trip was linked to another I made to Hawaii precisely two years earlier, on August 20, 2000. Together, the two trips served as a witness to me that God will confer a financial trust to Ephraim at the end of the age.

He *always* establishes a matter with two or more witnesses (Deuteronomy 19:15, 2 Corinthians 13:1).

During my original trip in August 2000, the Lord astounded me with a prophecy, given by Dr. Paula White, to the congregation at Word of Life Christian Center. I had no intentions of visiting any place of worship on that trip. Again, I thought was in Hawaii on business. I did not even know the church existed. Yet, that Sunday morning—through a series of wild unexpected circumstances—the Lord marshaled my daughter Ryan and me to Word of Life. I found myself sitting on a back pew just as Dr. White began to speak. She explained that God had instructed her to prophesy to the mid-morning congregation.

I sat there thunderstruck as God talked directly to me through her! As she prophesied, the Spirit of the Lord interpreted her message into a personal one for me. Dr. White spoke of a time, at the end of the age when God would release an extraordinary inheritance to His people for the spread of the gospel, as He smote "Egypt" with all His wonders. It would be a new season for the body of Christ. Many people would be "saved alive" in the last days, worldwide evangelical movement. Then, the end would come.

I carried the prophecy with me for 11 years, until it was tattered and torn in my briefcase. It took me that long to *fully* understand for whom the prophecy was meant. The message was intended for God's firstborn, Ephraim! When I first heard it, I knew nothing about Israel's lost tribes.

Ephraim's Divine Trust

The Lord's endowment to His people will support an unparalleled move of His Spirit to usher millions into His kingdom at the age's end. The movement will be financed by a valuable resource, crude oil, extracted from the earth by the Lord. At that time, the gift will be used to spread His precious gospel to desperate people, ensnared in a world spiraling out of control.

The descendants of the lost tribes of Ephraim are the inheritor of the divine estate. And for a good reason. Israel (Jacob), just before passing, gave Ephraim the blessing of the firstborn (Genesis 48:14). Thus, it will fall to Ephraim's descendants to handle the family's end-time trust.

God promised the Patriarchs that Ephraim would become a multitude in the midst of the earth. Today, she is just that! Although wayward for centuries, scattered to the nations in 722 B.C., and lost for nearly 3,000 years, Ephraim's "old dry bones" will be raised up to be bold and courageous witnesses for Yeshua Ha'Mashiach at the epoch's close!

And, at the *very* end, Ephraim shall be joined by his brethren, Judah (Ezekiel 37). A remnant of Judah (Jews) will survive the Great Tribulation. Ephraim and Judah—two parts of the same Olive Tree, God's two witnesses—will be united finally under the headship of Christ.

Scripture indicates the Josephs will be raised up as executors of Ephraim's estate, just as Joseph was elevated in his generation to oversee Egypt's storehouses during a time of great famine. The Josephs will manage the trust on behalf of Ephraim and the entire body of Christ.

On his deathbed, Israel spoke of this hidden heritance coming to Joseph and his offspring, Ephraim: *"And the Almighty who will bless you with blessings of heaven above, blessings of the deep that lies beneath …." (Genesis 49:22-26).*

Likewise, Moses proclaimed of Joseph, *"Blessed of the Lord is his land with the precious things of heaven, with the dew, and the deep lying beneath … with the precious things of earth and its fullness" (Deuteronomy 33:13-17).* Moses was not just speaking of Joseph's bountiful harvests of produce in coming seasons. God had something much larger in view—a more important harvest. He foresaw the Josephs' bountiful harvest of souls at the close of the Church Age!

God sent me all the way to Honolulu, Hawaii to put Dr. White's end-time prophecy in my hand. I returned to the Hawaiian Islands on business, quite unexpectedly, two years later, on the exact same day, August 20, 2002. It was no coincidence. On that trip, the Lord peeled back another tiny piece of the veil to reveal what the "precious blessing from beneath" was and from where it would come.

Don't Sell the Land!

During that second trip, my dad called to ask if I would sell him the land that he sold me as part of my inheritance many years earlier. At that time, he had been diagnosed with prostate cancer. It went into remission after six months of radiation treatments. Nevertheless, the diagnosis prompted him to consider what he would leave each of his children when he passed. By God's Providence, he chose to bequeath me the land he inherited as a young man from his long-deceased Aunt Bea and Uncle Zany.

Forever the businessman, my dad asked me to buy my bequest. I gladly purchased the land from him for $7,700, because my parents had no liquid assets at the time. The transaction gave me an excuse to help the two of them.

Even before I purchased the property from my father, God hinted it was quite valuable. I found an old contract in my father's documents, dating back to the time when my great aunt and uncle owned the land. It was a Mobil Oil lease. Mobil Oil leased the land for 10 years with the expectation of drilling for oil. But it never did, and eventually the contract expired. However, after I purchased the acreage from my father, all I seemed to do was pay taxes on it.

I had been paying taxes on the land for 11 years when my father asked to buy it back from me for the original $7,700. Someone had approached him to buy the 10 acres for $21,000. Since nothing had happened in the years I had it to prove its worth, and I liked to please my dad, I almost said yes. However, God taught me to pray first about everything.

On the morning of August 20, 2002, lying in my hotel bed, I asked the Lord if I should sell the land back to my father, so he could make a little profit. He told me not to sell the land under *any* circumstances. "That land is more valuable than anyone realizes," He warned.

My dad was not disappointed when I declined to sell back the estate. I explained to Him why. He encouraged me to investigate the matter.

Two days later, out of nowhere, I received a call from a British Petroleum (BP) executive. She wanted to engage my consulting services. We set an appointment to speak the next day. I thought nothing of our initial discussion. It was during our second telephone conversation that it began to dawn on me that God was pulling strings, arranging the chess pieces. After speaking to her that second time, I *knew* I was about to embark on an extraordinary journey. The outcome of that second call is recapped in the following journal excerpt.

August 23, 2002

The BP Connection

I just hung up the telephone with a high-ranking human resources executive and general manager at British Petroleum (BP). BP is the world's largest producer of oil and gas. Out of nowhere, the woman called two days ago to ask if I would come to Chicago on Monday, September 30, to talk to 100 of BP's highest-ranking executives. She wanted them to hear the Denny's Story and to see if I could help them on issues they were facing in their urban markets.

For my time, BP was prepared to donate to a charity of my choice. That was my original request. However, after listening to her talk, at length, about BP's streams of business, I realized this was not about my consulting services. God was setting me up! So, I made her a proposition. In exchange for my consulting services, I asked if BP would assign me a geo-scientist or engineer to consult with me about my property in Michigan. She accepted my offer.

What are the chances I would strike such a deal less than a week after God told me there was oil on my land? He promised He would orchestrate events for me to get it. He didn't waste any time. I cannot wait to see His next move!

At this point, the Lord needed to teach me more about Israel's 10 lost tribes, in time, referred to as Ephraim. He also wanted me to understand my relationship to these ancient people. As one of the Northern kingdom's largest tribes, Ephraim led many of the tribes into idolatry. Ephraim's capital, Samaria, is where many of Jacob's descendants became entwined in pagan worship and forsook God. They chose to worship false gods in Samaria rather than travel to Jerusalem—located in the Southern Kingdom of Judah—to worship the Lord.

Chapter 12
Something Samaritan is Going On!

A month after spending the day with BP's executives, the Lord gave me a dream, followed by a revelation that took my breath away. Together, they swept away any lingering doubt about the value of my land. God sealed the truth in my heart. There was oil on my estate! I had, indeed, inherited a priceless trust from my dad more valuable than anyone realized.

November 2, 2002

A Dream: Plowing for Hidden Treasure

In the dream, I was standing outside my house when a tall, thin man approached me. The man was dressed strangely. He wore a long dark tunic. The garment looked rough to the touch, as though it were made from the cloth of a potato sack. The man had long hair, high bony shoulders, and narrow feet. He said, "It's time to plow your yard." I had no idea my yard needed plowing.

The next thing I knew, he returned riding a big orange tractor. He made one, long diagonal swipe (northwest to southeast) across my wide land with the tractor. He plowed open a massive ditch. The ditch was filled with mounds of silver and gold coins the size of dinner plates!

I jumped down into the ditch and began scooping up the big coins. As I stacked several of the "coin-plates" in my arm, I decided I would run them through the dishwasher first. After that, I would take them to the bank for safekeeping.

I wanted the thin man to plow all my land to see if it held more buried treasure. Before I could ask him to do it, he disappeared. I searched for him everywhere. Finally, I spotted him entering a university or a school of some sort.

My dad and mom drove me to the school. I was frustrated with my dad because he could not park the car fast enough. "I have to catch this guy!" I yelled. Finally, he stopped the car. I leapt out of the backseat and rushed into the building. But the tall, thin man was gone. I could not find him anywhere.

I pondered the dream over and over in my head as I prayed to the Lord for understanding. Gradually, it dawned on me that the yard being plowed in my dream was not the grounds around my Memphis home. My home was surrounded by gardens. I did not have a lawn.

The land in the dream was the property I owned in Michigan, a wooded plot of 10 acres that butts my deceased uncle's estate. God told me the land was valuable, hinting at a hidden oil reserve. But before He released the treasure to me, I would have to learn many things, including who the trust was for and how to handle it for His glory. (Hence, my following Him into a university in the dream.)

Remembering the 1960s television show, *The Beverly Hillbillies*, I teased: "Ishi, You're going to have to give me this oil like You gave it to Jed Clampett. You've got to put it in my lap." In the dream, the treasure was extracted for me. With one swift tractor swipe, the priceless fortune was exposed. My only role was to collect and bank the booty. Little did I know at the time of the dream that a single seismic line, cut on the same northwest-southeast diagonal as in my dream, would reveal activity on my land about a mile beneath the earth's surface! Usually, geologists must conduct multiple seismic lines to discover a possible deposit.

An astonishing revelation, related to this extraordinary dream, came less than two days later. God would use the dream and the revelation to open my eyes to the ancient Samaritans and their modern-day descendants.

November 4, 2002

The Mystery of the Samaritan Woman

The strangest thing happened last night as I prepared for bed. As I walked through the private hallway to my bedroom, I was drawn to a painting I bought in Ethiopia. It was a lovely original painting of Yeshua with the Samaritan woman at the well. It cost me a small fortune, an impulse purchase for Ryan. I acquired it because it reminded me of a chapter in her book, Saving Grace.

In that beloved chapter, Grace, who was not yet a believer, was talking to Mike, her future husband, about the Samaritan woman. Grace just did not get the Living Water concept. Mike, a believer, patiently explained the text to her. Mike, whose name means "like God" in Hebrew, was a type of Christ in the book. For this reason, I purchased the portrait, and then regretted it when the bills came rolling in from that trip.

While Ryan liked the picture, she did not want a Biblical work of art hanging in her bedroom or home office, so I stored it in my garage in the shipping crate. One day, I would donate it to a church.

When it came time to move Ryan to her new downtown apartment, I needed the shipping crate to transport another large picture to her place. Had that need not arisen, I am not sure I would have ever taken the canvas out of the crate.

Once out, I decided to hang the portrait in the hallway, leading to my bedroom. The longer it hung there, the more I liked it. I never paid too much attention to it until last night. Drawn to the picture, I began to study it closely.

For the first time, I noticed the Samaritan woman was dressed in the national dress of an Ethiopian woman. I ran to my closet to get the one given to me as a gift on my last trip. I compared my dress to the one in the portrait. They could be the same dress.

Then my eyes moved to the Lord, who sat on the well as He spoke to the woman. He was tall and thin. His hair rested on His high bony shoulders. His elongated feet protruded underneath His rough-looking tunic. I gasped, "HE'S THE MAN IN MY DREAM!" The Man in the portrait and the Man in my dream, who plowed my land and unearthed the fortune, were one and the same—Yeshua!

While I found the connection wildly fascinating to ponder, I did not understand why the Lord would approach me about an oil reserve on my land, using a portrait of the Samaritan woman. Deep in my spirit, I sensed a hidden connection between the Samaritan and me.

Over the next few days, as I gazed at the portrait, the Lord reminded me of a long-ago event that happened when I lived in Miami. Up until that time, I thought I had just done a good deed, nothing more. Only four people in the world knew what I had done: my daughter, who was seven years old at the time; Fayoola, her friend who was a year older than she; Jerry, the man I helped; and me.

Now I saw the event in a whole new light. God led me to respond to a stranger in the way I did that day to drive home a point: I was a modern-day Samaritan, part Jew, part Gentile. I was a descendant of the ancient Samaritans!

November 7, 2002

The Good Samaritan

I am now completely convinced Yeshua wants me to identify with the Samaritan people because I am a descendant. Last night, as I pondered all that God was showing me about Ephraim, He reminded me of an experience I had in 1988, which mirrored that of the Good Samaritan in the Bible.

I helped a guy, but that was not what was unusual. I help a lot of people. It was the way in which I helped this man. I did what the Good Samaritan did in the Bible. I remember the incident as if it were yesterday.

I walked into my room at Wayside early to set up my Sunday school materials. I was both the teacher and director. As soon as I walked in, I noticed a visitor sitting in the back. He and I were the only two people in the room. I welcomed him. Soon others joined us.

There were several visitors that day, but this man stood out because he had a white, blood-stained bandage wrapped around his head. When it came time, I asked the visitors to stand and introduce themselves, so we could welcome them.

The man's name was Jerry. He was a tall, lanky white guy from Dallas, Texas. He spoke slowly with a deep Southern drawl.

I taught the lesson and from the expression on Jerry's face, I could tell he enjoyed it. After that, we all went to the worship service. I savored every moment. Right after church, the Singles Department had planned a spaghetti luncheon in the gym for the whole congregation. After we fed the hungry multitudes, we all went home for a few hours. Some members of the class took Jerry with them.

Everyone showed up again for prayer and the evening worship service around 5:30 p.m. The evening service, which was quite inspiring, ended around 8:30 p.m. People began leaving. I remained to talk to some members of my class. We talked until they started turning out the lights. I wrapped up my conversation and headed for the exit.

I had been conversing at the front of the church. When I reached the back of the sanctuary, I saw Jerry sitting in the middle of the last pew. I asked him how he enjoyed the day. I told him I was delighted that he could spend the whole day with us. He assured me he had enjoyed being around us. I said, "Well, it's time to go home." That's when he informed me that he had no place to go. He told me his story as we exited the sanctuary.

That very morning, Jerry arrived in Miami from Dallas by Greyhound Bus. As soon as he got off the bus, eight black men mugged him. They took everything he had—his wallet, baggage, clothes, and shoes. They left him naked, on the ground, bleeding from the head.

Shortly after that, a man came along with clothes and shoes in the trunk of his car. He had planned to donate the items to Goodwill. He gave Jerry the clothing instead. Everything fit, including the shoes! Someone also helped bandage his head and gave him a lift to Wayside. That is why he was sitting in class so early when I arrived.

By the time Jerry finished his story, everyone had left the church grounds. The parking lot was empty except my daughter Ryan, her friend Fayoola, Jerry, and me. So, we all piled in my car and I took Jerry to my bank across from Dadeland Mall.

I took $125 from the ATM machine and gave it to him. Then, I drove him to Howard Johnson's on U.S. 1 and checked him in. I gave the manager my credit card. I told him to let Jerry stay there for as long as needed and to charge my account. The manager made an imprint of my card. I signed the blank imprint.

The manager gave Jerry the room key and we drove him around to his unit to make sure he got in safely. By this time, his head ached, and he complained of dizziness. He was also starting to have memory issues. I gave Jerry my work telephone number in case he needed anything. I encouraged him to rest and not be concerned about the tab. He needed time to recuperate.

After Jerry checked out a week later, the hotel manager charged his room to my American Express card and sent me the bill. Upon receipt of the bill, I called the manager. He informed me Jerry had taken a bus back to Dallas.

After I helped Jerry, the devil convinced me that my husband, Mike, would find out about the incident and accuse me of having an affair. I could just hear accusations: "What's this bill for? Why are you paying for a motel? Are you having an affair?"

Strangely enough, a man did, in fact, leave a telephone message for Jerry, accusing him of having an affair with his wife. Jerry, a committed Christian, was quite upset by the message and called me at work in Miami to see if my husband was angry about my helping him. I assured him the call did not come from my husband since Mike knew nothing of the incident.

After Jerry's call, I became filled with an irrational fear that Mike would, indeed, somehow learn about what I had done. I would have hell to pay. However, the Lord got me alone in a small second-floor room just before the Wednesday night church service. He gently reasoned with me. In an instant, He supernaturally took away the fear. Suddenly calmed, I sobbed uncontrollably. Rivers of gratitude poured from my eyes. His assurances of protection gave me the relief I needed.

Now I knew that incident was not random. God orchestrated it years ago to demonstrate a point that He would make in the coming years about who I was. I was a modern-day offspring of the despised Samaritans of Jesus' day! However, I was not alone. Millions of others could make the same claim. Only God knew *who* we were and *where* we were.

This was just the beginning. The Lord would teach me much more about my ancestors, who resided in the ancient capital of Samaria in Northern Israel. Over the course of time, the Samaritan name became interchangeable with Israel's most prominent tribe, Ephraim. In time, these residents of the northern part of Israel became known as Samaritans!

The Lord taught me about these people as He prepared to extract the trust that "lay beneath" for their descendants, whom He would restore to Himself for Himself. I will never forget how He delivered the news to me one night that many African Americans were a part of this sacred lineage.

November 6, 2002

"Everyone Will Wear Black and White"

In the middle of the day on Monday, my assistant, Claudia, left me a voicemail message: "Oh, by the way, Patty Dexter told me to tell you that for Women's Day everyone will wear black and white." That tidbit of information was more important than she knew.

*The last time I spoke at a Women's Day observance was in Greenville, South Carolina. The whole congregation wore white, even the men! No one told me white was the order of the day, so I showed up in a red business suit. But I could see God's hand in the congregation's attire. No one knew my topic but Him. He gave it to me—*The Glorious Bride of Christ. *As I took the podium and looked out at the congregation, all I could see was a sea of white. These worshippers looked just like a glorious bride!*

Now, debriefing my day with Yeshua that night, I finally hit upon the topic of the black and white dress for the Women's Day observance in Detroit. I would be the keynote speaker at Overcomers Evangel Church that Sunday. Thinking back to my South Carolina experience, I asked, "Why are they wearing black and white?" Yeshua loves symbolism, so I suspected there was a reason. I had the answer before I could finish the sentence. I started to scream.

"I know why! I know why!" I could hear Him laughing beneath my screams.

"Why? Why?" He urged me on.

"BECAUSE THEY ARE A MIXED PEOPLE! LIKE ME, THEY ARE DESCENDANTS OF THE SAMARITANS!" It spilled out of me. I could not stop screaming.

The puzzle pieces tumbled into place. "Oh, my goodness! That means those Detroiters are descendants of Ephraim—the lost tribes of Ephraim ... Israel!" I yelled. "So...many African American believers are descendants of the 10 northern tribes of Israel! They're the ones whose ancestors were strewn to the nations because of idolatry? It's THEIR song? It's THEIR song I'll sing?" I could hardly contain myself. God told me one day, I would "sing" (i.e., share) Ephraim's story of sorrow with the world.[3]

The Lord was just as excited as I about my discovery. He loves it when I connect His dots. I had suspected a link between African Americans and Israel's 10 lost tribes, but I could not figure it out. I knew of the tie between African Americans and Judah, because of my own Ethiopian Jewish heritage.

My mind raced back and forth across the centuries ... the millennia. How did the descendants of Ephraim (Israel) end up in the United States as believers in Christ? I decided to begin at the beginning, melding together what I knew about Biblical, African, and African American history.[4]

Tracking the Lineage of the True Israelites Through History:

1. *God created Adam and Eve, who had three sons—Cain, Abel, and Seth (Gen. 1:26-27, 4:1-2, 25). Through the line of Seth came seven generations and then the Great Flood in Noah's day (Gen. 5).*
2. *Noah had three sons—Shem, Ham, and Japheth—from whom all the nations of the earth descended after the Great Flood (Gen. 6:9-10, 10:32).*
3. *Through the line of Japheth came Gomer (Indo Europeans), Magog (Russians), Madai (Medes), Javan (Greeks), Tubal, Meschech and Tiras (Gen. 10:2-5).*

---

[3]*Ephraim's song is a ballad of suffering and woe. The Lord explained that at this juncture in my life, I had not suffered enough, and therefore, was not yet qualified to tell Ephraim's story. He assured me, however, the time would come when I would be qualified. Relatedly, in February 2011, the Lord gave me a dream in which I heard a melodious male voice singing a refrain from James Weldom Johnson's* Lift Evr'y Voice and Sing. *Later, the Lord explained this was Ephraim's song! See Appendix for lyrics.*
[4]*See Appendix for detailed lineage charts.*

4. *Through the line of Ham came the Black African nations: Cush (Kush or Ethiopians), Mizraim (Egyptians), Phut or Put, and Canaan (Canaanites) (Gen. 10:6-20).*
5. *Through the line of Shem came the Hebrews (Gen. 10:21-31).*
6. *Shem begot Elam, Asshur (Assyrians), Axphaxad, Lud (Lydia), and Aram (Syrians) (Gen. 10: 22). Axphaxad begot Salah, who begot Eber, who begot, Peleg, who begot Reu, who begot Serug, who begot Nahor, who begot Terah, who begot Abraham, Nabor, and Haran (Gen. 11:10-26).*
7. *God called Abraham, the Patriarch of the Hebrews, to leave Ur and sojourn to Canaan—the land He would give His people (Gen. 11:31-12:1-5).*
8. *Abraham and his wife Sarah bore Isaac (Gen. 17:16, 19, 21:1-7). Isaac was the son of the promise (Gal..4:21-31), not Ishmael, whom Abraham had with Sarah's Egyptian handmaiden, Hagar (Gen. 16:15, 17:19-21).*
9. *Isaac bore two sons (twins)—Esau and Jacob—with Rebekah (Gen. 25:21-26). Jacob deceived Esau out of his birthright, so the promise passed to Jacob's line (Gen. 25:29-34, 27:1-40), while Esau became the forefather of the Edomites (Gen. 36).*
10. *Jacob, whom God renamed Israel, had 12 sons through Leah, Rachel, and their handmaidens, Zilpah and Bilhah, respectively (Gen. 29:31-34, 30:1-24).*
11. *Joseph, Jacob's favorite son through Rachel, was hated by his brothers, who sold him into Egyptian slavery (Gen. 37:3-4, 12-36).*
12. *God raised up Joseph in Egypt to become second to Pharaoh, serving as his viceroy or governor (Gen. 41:40-41).*
13. *Joseph married the Egyptian High Priest's daughter, Asenath (Gen. 41:45). The ancient Egyptians—descendants of "Mizraim"—were Hamitic (Black) people (Gen. 10:6).*
14. *Joseph and Asenath had two sons—Manasseh and Ephraim (Gen. 41:40-41), who were Semitic and Hamitic (Hebrew and Black).*[5]

---

[5]*Hebrews were often mistaken for Egyptians—a Hamatic, dark-skinned people. For example, Joseph's brothers believed he was a native Egyptian when they sought food in Egypt during the famine (Genesis 42:1-8). The entire company (Hebrew and Egyptian) that buried Jacob in Canaan were mistaken for Egyptians (Genesis 50:7-11). Moses was mistaken for an Egyptian by the priest of Midian's seven daughters (Exodus 2:19). Even the Apostle Paul was mistaken for an Egyptian by Claudias Lysias, the commander of the Roman garrison (Acts 21:38).*

15. *Israel, his wives, and their 12 sons, with all their families moved to Egypt to be near Joseph during the famine. Over the course of four centuries, Israel's family of 70 (66 from Canaan and four in Joseph's family) grew into 12 tribes, representing the nation of Israel (Gen. 46:26).*
16. *Israel, on his deathbed, gave Joseph a double blessing by giving Joseph's sons, Manasseh and Ephraim, Joseph's position as firstborn (Gen. 48:12-22).*[6]
17. *Manasseh (Joseph's literal firstborn) and Ephraim (blessed by Israel as the firstborn) came to represent two of Israel's 12 tribes, further incorporating Hamitic people into the line of Shem (Num. 1:32-34).*
18. *Israel's act of crossing his hands to place his right hand on the head of Ephraim during his final blessing, elevated Ephraim, unequivocally, to the status of firstborn that had significant implications for all succeeding generations, including ours (Jer. 31:9).*
19. *In time, the Israelites' numbers threatened the Egyptians, so they enslaved the Hebrews. Undoubtedly, many more in Shem's line became "mixed people" (Semitic and Hamitic) as a result of this enslavement that lasted more than four centuries.*[7]
20. *After 430 years of slavery, God raised up Moses to lead the Hebrews out of Egyptian slavery to Canaan, the Promised Land. Many Egyptians sojourned with the Israelites (Ex. 12:38, Num. 11:4). The trek took 40 years. This created more opportunities to blend Semitic and Hamitic lines.*
21. *Joshua led the children of these Israelites into the Promised Land of Canaan, conquering the pagan Canaanites, who represented many Hamitic peoples (Jos. 1:1-24).*
22. *The Israelites did not conquer all the land God promised them (i.e., territories of the Canaanites, Hittites, Amorites, Perizzites, Havities, and Jebusites). As a consequence, many of the Israelites became entangled in mixed marriages with*

---

[6]*Reuben was Israel's literal firstborn.*

[7]*American slavery serves as an example of how slave masters and slaves mingled to create generations of blended offspring.*

the Canaanites (Ez. 9), who remained in the land, producing more dark-skinned (and pagan) offspring.

23. *After the death of Solomon, God split Israel into two kingdoms—the Northern kingdom, comprised of the 10 northern tribes and the Southern kingdom, comprised of Judah and Benjamin (1 Kings 11-12, 2 Chron. 10).*
24. *The tribe of Ephraim (a single tribe in the beginning) settled in the northern territory of Israel. Ephraim grew to become one of Israel's largest, most prominent tribes.*
25. *Over the course of time, both kingdoms became idolatrous, influenced and ensnared by the pagan nations around them.*
26. *The Northern kingdom, at different points in history was referred to as Ephraim, Samaria, and Israel.*
27. *Further along in its waywardness from God than the Southern kingdom, God used the Assyrians to conquer and scatter the northern tribes in 722 B.C.*
28. *Roughly 50 years later, the king of Assyria sent foreigners from other conquered nations to settle Israel's northern territory. These foreigners intermarried with the poor Hebrews who remained there, creating a people who were to become known in Christ's day as the Samaritans. They mixed their worship of the Lord with other pagan religions. The Judeans considered the Samaritans a mongrel, pagan race, to be greatly despised.*
29. *In 586 B.C., 136 years after the Assyrians conquered the Northern kingdom, God allowed the Babylonians to take the Southern kingdom (Judah and Benjamin) into exile for 70 years (Jer. 29:10, Dan. 9:2).*
30. *The Persians conquered the Babylonians in 539 B.C. The Persian king, Cyrus the Great, sent a remnant of Jews back to Jerusalem to rebuild the temple, wall, and city. However, the vast majority of Jews remained in Persia and its surrounding provinces.*
31. *The returning remnant remained in Israel through the 400 years of God's silence (i.e., from the close of the Book of Malachi to the opening of the Book of Matthew).*
32. *Christ then entered human history as a little Jewish Baby. He grew up to be a Man and was revealed to be Messiah. But He was rejected by the Judeans, who loathed Him and the half-breed Samaritans, living in the north.*

33. *Christ was crucified. God resurrected Him after three days. After 40 days, He ascended into heaven to sit at God's right side to serve as our King and High Priest. He shall come again to judge the wicked (see Matthew, Mark, Luke, and John).*
34. *God judged the Judeans in 70 A.D. because they missed the time of Christ's visitation. The Roman General, Titus, marched into Jerusalem and destroyed the temple, which was no longer needed as God's Spirit now resided within His people.*[8]
35. *Titus murdered masses during his invasion of Jerusalem. The surviving Jews fled to Samaria and other parts beyond.*
36. *The Judeans and Samaritans were eventually dispersed throughout the nations of the world as were the other 10 tribes by the Assyrians nearly 800 years earlier.*
37. *In a migration that took approximately 1,200 years, some of Israel's heritage journeyed south through Egypt and Ethiopia, across sub-Saharan Africa to the West Coast of Africa. There, they built three pagan empires—Ghana, Mali, and Songhai.*
38. *Thus, Shem's heritage was eventually taken on slave ships to the Western Hemisphere as judgment for their idolatry. This re-enslavement ("back to Egypt") was prophesied by Moses in Deuteronomy 28:15-68.*[9] *In Hosea 11:9-11b, the prophet predicted Ephraim would come back to Israel "trembling from the west" ... "like a bird from Egypt" at the end of the age.*
39. *In slavery, the descendants of the Hebrews lost their Hebrew identity. It was customary for the slavers to place a curse on each departing ship filled with slaves. They swore oaths that the slaves would forget their homeland, families, and*

---

[8]*After Christ's resurrection, a physical temple was no longer needed. The believer's physical body becomes the temple of the Holy Spirit of the Lord (1 Corinthians 6:19-20). The Lord writes His law in our hearts and minds as the Old Testament prophets foretold He would (Isaiah 59:21, Jeremiah 31:33-35; also, see Hebrews 10:16).*

[9]*It is critical to note the Israelites were never taken on slave ships during the Assyrian or Babylonian invasions. There was no need. Israel shared the same land mass as their invaders! Further, the Judeans dispersed by Rome in 70 A.D., throughout the Middle East, Central and Southern Africa, Western and Eastern Europe, Southwestern Asia, India, and China, were never taken on slave ships for the same reason. Jacob's seed was taken on slave ships during the Transatlantic Slave Trade, which began in the 1,400s and lasted four centuries.*

ancestors. They decreed the captives would, in effect, lose their identities, which is exactly what happened.[10]

40. *After four centuries of brutal slavery, many of Israel's progeny turned to Christ. They grew to become a mixed multitude (half Hebrew, half Gentile) hidden within His body. They claim Him as Messiah. They are hidden (not lost) within the nations of the world. (See Chapter 2: "Mystery of the Hidden Treasure.") They will be raised up and revived at the end of the age from the graveyard of the nations to become an exceedingly great army of witnesses for Christ (Eze. 37 and Rev. 7:1-8, 14:1-5).*

I found it beyond interesting to later discover that the overwhelming majority of Jews in the land of Israel—the Ashkenazi Jews, who represent roughly 80 percent of Israel's population—are descendants of Noah's son, Japaheth, not Shem! Jacob, renamed Israel by God, is a direct descendant of Shem through Eber (Genesis 10:21, 35:10). Eber was the ancestor of Abraham, after whom the Hebrews are named.

According to Genesis 10:2-5, the Ashkenaz people descended specifically from Gomer, and it states clearly that they are among the "coastland peoples of the Gentiles" (emphasis mine):

> *The sons of Japheth were Gomer, Magog, Madai, Javan, Tubal, Meshech, and Tiras. The sons of Gomer were* ***ASHKENAZ****, Riphath, and Togarmah. The sons of Javan were Elishah, Tarshish, Kittim, and Dodanim.* ***FROM THESE THE COASTLAND PEOPLES OF THE GENTILES WERE SEPARATED*** *into their lands, everyone according to his language, according to their families, into their nations.*

---

[10]*This does not mean that all Americans of African descent are descendants of Jacob (Israel). A person must come from the line of Jacob to be a true descendant. It is likely other peoples of African descent, presently residing in some territories of Africa and in nations effected by the Transatlantic Slave Trade (e.g., West Indies) are also a part of Israel's generations.*

The Scythians, a nomadic tribe that settled in the Eurasian Steppe Region between the Black and Caspian Seas are descendants of the Ashkenaz. During the eighth and seventh centuries, they migrated to Southern Russia and eventually populated Northwest Europe. Surely, the Ashkenazi Jews—identified as the progeny of Gentile peoples in God's Word—converted to Judaism at some point in history. Some believe the conversion was around 740 A.D., led by King Bulan of the Khazars. This view is hotly disputed by others.

After this stunning discovery, a New Testament Scripture passage I had read dozens of times and puzzled over for years, suddenly took on meaning: *"Indeed I will make those of the synagogue of Satan, who say they are Jews and are not, but lie—indeed I will make them come and worship before your feet, and to know that I have loved you" (Revelation 3:9).* Christ spoke these words to the faithful Church of Philadelphia. This body of believers kept the Lord's Word and His command to persevere, although they were weak. Of these faithful believers who never denied His name, He promised: *"I also will keep you from the hour of trial which shall come upon the whole world, to test those who dwell on the earth" (Revelation 3:10).* This verse refers to the Great Tribulation.

Sephardic Jews, who represent nearly 20 percent of Israel's present population, are indigenous to the Middle East. They were in Israel in 70 A.D. when the Romans overthrew Jerusalem, and they are direct descendants of Noah's son, Shem. However, many historians believe they are largely the descendants of Esau—Jacob's twin brother—progeny of the Edomites.

According to Genesis 36:8-9, the Edomites lived in the Seir Mountains. They were driven north by the Nabateans, a nomadic tribe of ancient Arab people, to the area around southern Judah and Hebron, called Idumea during the Greco-Roman period. They intermarried with many of the true Israelites. They learned their ways, adopted their customs, and in due course, were absorbed into the Judean culture. In fact, intermarriage is how Antipater, governor of Idumea, was made procurer of Judea, Samaria, and Galilee by the Roman Emperor Julius Caesar, paving the way to the throne for his son, Herod the Great.

Some theologians believe the Edomites assisted the Romans in the butchery and scattering of the true Israelites in 70 A.D., during the destruction of Jerusalem and the second temple. The Book of Obadiah may lend some support to this argument. In Obadiah 1:1-21, the prophet speaks of a final judgment on Edom's descendants during the Day of the Lord. The judgment traces to a treachery against his brother Jacob during the time of Jacob's calamity—"when foreigners entered his gates and cast lots for Jerusalem" ... "in the day of his captivity" ... "in the day of their destruction" (vv. 10-15).

After 70 A.D., the Edomites who remained after the temple and Jerusalem were destroyed, migrated to Spain and Portugal, where they lived for centuries peacefully among Christians and Muslims. In these regions, they became known as Sephardim or Sephardic Jews. However, when they were expelled from Spain in 1492 by King Ferdinand and Queen Isabella, those who refused to convert to Catholicism or who were not executed, resettled in Middle Eastern and North African communities, eventually migrating to Israel.

Discovering Modern-Day Samaritans

Just a few short weeks after revealing to me that many of today's American believers of African descent were the progeny of the ancient Samaritans, descendants of Jacob (Israel), God moved in an extraordinary way to show me more about this wonder. He orchestrated a sweet surprise for me. I never saw it coming. I did not realize what was happening until I was in the midst of it. I will always treasure that Sunday at Temple of Deliverance when God opened my eyes to the truth about His people in a very personal way.

November 24, 2002

My Sweet Samaritan Surprise

I suspected nothing when Bishop G.E. Patterson began to speak this morning on the topic of the ten lepers. His subject was taken from Luke 17:11-19. Before he began the sermon, he told us he would speak from a familiar text. "Everybody has probably heard the story a hundred times," he said. "Everybody but the 'unchurched.'" I surmised I was in for a treat when he said only one of the ten lepers— the Samaritan—returned to thank Christ for his healing.

The Bishop began his sermon by telling the congregation how the Jews and Samaritans went to great lengths to avoid each other, to segregate themselves, mainly because of their religious differences and practices. He explained that the three cities—Galilee, Samaria, and Jerusalem—were on the same side of the Jordan River. Galilee was located near Samaria and Samaria near Jerusalem.

A Jew traveling from Jerusalem to Galilee or from Galilee to Jerusalem would cross the Jordan River to avoid going through Samaria. When the traveler neared or reached his city of destination, he would cross back over the Jordan River. He pointed out, however, that in living with the sickness and stigmatism of leprosy, the ten lepers (nine Jews and one Samaritan) banded together. They were all outcasts of society.

The text spoke of how Jesus was on His way to Jerusalem, and as he traveled along the border between Samaria and Galilee, he encountered the ten lepers. They cried out to Him for mercy. He counseled them to go show themselves to the priests, in keeping with Mosaic Law. Only the priests could pronounce them clean and allow them to return to their communities and families.

By faith, marked with visible sores, scabs, and scars, the ten lepers made their way to the priests. They were healed en route. Their body parts regenerated as they moved by faith in Christ's word. The faith of those lepers made the congregation crazy with praise—even though they had heard the story 100 times before. Only the Samaritan, the most unlikely one—"the foreigner"—returned to give Christ thanks for his healing.

By the time the Bishop got to that part, the entire congregation was on its feet. Spontaneous praise poured forth. Music began. Hundreds of people were screaming and crying about the goodness and faithfulness of God. They saw themselves in the story. God had been good to them too. In their times of trouble, He had performed miracles for them as He had done for the lepers.

They gave loud thanks with raised hands and shouts. The few who were seated could no longer remain so. They jumped to their feet and joined the jubilation. Some congregants danced; others ran around the sanctuary in unrestrained expressions of gratitude for what Christ had done in their lives.

Suddenly, my eyes were opened!

Tears sprang to my eyes as I realized what I was watching. No one else in the room caught it—at least no one visible. But I did! Right before my very eyes, in that very space, were the descendants of the Samaritans celebrating, crying, and shouting thanks to God for what He had done in their lives.

Many in that sanctuary, like the Samaritan in the story, were poor outcasts, living on the lowest rungs of society. But they were grateful to God for the ways He had demonstrated His love for them, for the ways He had shown up in the lives to right wrongs, soothe injuries, and bind up their wounds. He had performed countless miracles in the lives. And, as it was with the lepers, these marvels had gone mostly unnoticed by mainstream society.

Bishop Patterson could no longer speak. Like everyone else, he too, was overcome with gratitude and joy. He motioned for Mother Pelt to take the podium. As he took his seat, he wiped the tears from his eyes.

Mother Pelt, a deaconess in the church, rose. About 70 years old, she had a glowing reputation as a powerful Bible teacher. Every Sunday, she sat on the platform with the rest of the bishops.

The meticulously dressed, petite elderly woman took the podium. She was attired in a bold black and white suit. The dramatic pattern caught my attention. Instantly, I made the connection. The black and white symbolized her mixed heritage! But she did not know it. She encouraged the congregation to continue giving praise to God.

I noticed the bishops behind her on stage. Standing with raised hands, they were all dressed in their usual black and white clergy uniforms.

My eyes traveled further back, and I noticed the large male choir standing and praising God in the choir loft. They were all dressed in black suits with white shirts! Many wore black and white ties to match their suits. Next, I noticed all the deacons at the head of each section in the front pews. Standing and praising God. They, too, wore black and white! The nurses, who always sat in the first four pews in the front and left of the sanctuary, were standing in their white uniforms, over which they wore short black capes.

I glanced at my daughter to the right of me. Standing, clapping, and giving praise to God, she was dressed in black and white. I had not realized it until that very moment. (Later, she told me she almost changed her clothes, but decided at the last minute to keep on the outfit she wore.)

My eyes traveled to the young lady to the left of me, who was standing, rocking, and sobbing into a wad of tissues. She, too, was dressed in black and white with a beautiful black velvet hat on her

> *head! I pulled out my own big wad of tissues and joined her as I continued to survey the sanctuary in awe. There I was, standing amid "the foreigners!" The most unlikely ones were giving unrestrained, high praise to God Almighty for His mercy and goodness in their lives!*

These were His witnesses! God had performed a quiet miracle in my life that day to teach me an important truth. Scripture was unfolding right there before my very eyes. That day, I looked up to heaven in awe: "Oh Lord, how Your heart must burst with joy and pride to finally see Israel's descendants praising Your holy name, giving witness to Your power and goodness!" Nothing could contain my joy at that point.

Chapter 13
Drilling for Treasure

On April 4, 2003, my parents and I, with the help of John Manner, a geologist referred to us by BP, established our own limited liability oil and gas company, The Ephraim Project. Three years later, we changed the name to Ephraim Oil and Gas, after I formed a private foundation to help the poor and named it The Ephraim Project.

My parents and I aggressively pushed for the right to drill a well on our land. Relatives, with whom we held 21 acres of the land "Tenants in Common", blocked us from drilling on our 10 acres for nearly three years. We could go forward only if we made them partners in the business, which God forbade. So, we were forced to fight the matter in court. We battled all the way up, just short of the Michigan Supreme Court. After two prolonged court battles, the judge divided the land between four families, giving us the right to drill on our acreage.

What no one knew, not even my family, was I had no money to drill. Only God knew I lacked the resources, and He did not seem a bit flustered, so I was not either. By this time, I was $750,000 in debt, down from the $1.1 million. And although I made $31,250 a month, I lived paycheck to paycheck, due in part to the hefty pre-drilling expenses and litigation costs.

Based on John Manner's conservative estimates, I needed $471,000 to drill. I was not concerned about this staggering sum because God had already performed miracle after miracle to get me to the point where I was. I could not have come that far without Him. Surely, He would see me through to the end.

The various contractors on the other end had no idea Ephraim Oil and Gas was essentially a single, black woman in Orlando, Florida, living paycheck to paycheck. All they knew was Ephraim Oil and Gas paid its bills on time, even before time. I operated as if I was a large firm with resources.

No matter the amount of an invoice—$2,000, $5,000, $15,000, even $25,000—God would always put the money in my hands. After so many of these instances, I was confident when it came time to drill that He would, once again, put the money in my hand.

It was summer 2005, when the Lord began to speak to me about how I would get the funds to drill. It would be tricky. I would have to obey His instructions to the letter.

August 9, 2005

A Dream: "Cash Out!"

For the past several days, I have teased the Lord relentlessly about "making a move" so I could make a move to speed up my life: "Ishi, it's Your move! My Ishi's got moves! Can we move this thing along, Ishi?"

"Making moves" was the major theme of last Sunday's sermon at New Destiny. Last night—August 8, 2005 at 10:39 p.m.—God made a move! He gave me a dream.

The dream opened with me standing next to Denny's General Counsel, Rhonda Parish. She instructed me to do something: "Close out on the twelfth one." I had no idea what she was talking about. She told me again, "Close everything out on the twelfth." I still did not understand what I was supposed to do.

Then Nelson Marchioli, the president, popped up in the dream to clarify her instructions: "Cash it all out on the twelfth." As Nelson spoke, I saw a vision of a ledger with a zero balance on it ("0.00").

Finally, I understood the "twelfth one" was a date. I said, "Oh, the twelfth refers to a date." Also, I knew whatever I was supposed to do on the twelfth involved three packages.

Suddenly, I woke up, groggy. "Liquidate on the twelfth," I spoke out loud to my empty hotel room. I simply recited what I last heard in my spirit before fully waking. With my eyes still closed I asked, "Ishi, what do you mean liquidate on the twelfth?" Then my eyes sprung open. I shot straight up in the bed.

"Oh no, I can't!" I realized what He was asking me to do. I protested, "That's too close, Ishi!" Then I came to my senses. I held my tongue. I did not want to say another thing—something else wrong.

The Lord was instructing me to cash out three of my four stock packages on the twelfth of September! The twelfth of August was only four days away. The paperwork simply could not be processed that quickly, so He must have been referring to September. Up until that dream, I had never considered cashing in my stock options because I thought the packages that I held were worthless.

As I studied the packages, I discovered I was wrong. I also knew exactly which three to cash out—the three with the trading value of $5 to $6. The fourth package would require a stock price well above $10 to become valuable. (I never benefited from the fourth package. The options expired before ever reaching the option price.)

The window to cash out stock for employees (or me) closed on the twelfth of September at the trading bell. After that, we were not allowed to trade until the next window three months later. If I conducted a transaction outside the window, I could be accused of insider trading. This carried stiff penalties.

In my mind, the twelfth was cutting it too close. Why not cash out sometime in mid-to-late August or during the first week of September? Why did I have to wait until the last day? And why cash out all three? At the current trading price, one package had the potential to cover the cost of the drilling. Why not let the other two become more valuable with time?

I had a lot of questions. It seemed more prudent to do it just a little bit differently than what the Lord instructed. But after my initial outburst, I made a conscious decision not to question His directive.

I recalled examples in Scripture of God giving people strange and odd instructions. How could marching around the walls of a city for six days—seven times on the seventh day—blowing a trumpet and shouting, flatten a city's walls? How could washing seven times in the dirty Jordan River cleanse a man of leprosy? How could a man find money to pay his taxes by going fishing? (Peter found money to pay his temple tax in the mouth of a fish!)

In God's economy, faith matters. Faith makes things happen. It moves God's hand. Those who obey His commands are big winners. Those who do not, lose big. That morning, I resolved to move by faith. Regardless of what I felt was the right thing to do, I would obey the Lord's command.

I became especially determined to do so after I reread my notes from Sunday's sermon on having a "right-now faith." Incidentally, I happened to have the sermon notes with me on that business trip. In the sermon message, there was a sense of urgency to MOVE! Also, I found a lyric from a Bill Withers' song on the few journal pages I brought with me on the trip. They tickled me: *"Good things come to those who wait, but not to those who wait too late."*

It was my move. I made a note to call Kelly Land, Denny's stock administrator, for an appointment as soon as I was back home. I would arrange to cash out three of my four stock packages on September 12, 2005.

I should mention five hours after the Lord gave me the dream, instructing me to cash out, He gave me a vision. The vision commanded me to possess the land. It tied to the dream:

August 9, 2005

A Vision: Possess the Land!

I had a vision before dawn, exactly at 3:30 a.m. In the vision, two people were standing on either side of me. I was sitting in a chair between them. They showed me something folded in a newspaper. They lowered the paper carefully so I could see it.

Before I saw it, I heard it. I heard dirt or sand pouring. Upon hearing the sound, I said, "Oh, it's land!" That declaration did not mean a thing to me until I woke up.

Upon waking, the words "possess the land" came into my spirit. At first, I thought the Lord was referring to land I wanted to buy for a family compound in Orlando when we came into oil. Then suddenly I knew He was referring to the earth. God instructed His people to occupy the land—take dominion of the earth—for His sake until Christ returned. Somehow, cashing out my stock on the twelfth of September with Kelly LAND had something to do with possessing the LAND until Christ returned.

Three days after the dream, I telephoned Kelly Land to make the necessary arrangements to cash in three of my four stock options. I told her I would come to her office the following week to sign the papers. I had no idea what the stock prices would be on the twelfth of September, a month away. God knew I had made a deliberate decision to detach myself from the rise and fall of Denny's stock. I had to trust Him. Kelly and I agreed that unless I gave her a call, and I knew I would not, she was to cash out all three packages on September 12—no matter what.

The day I had the dream, I told Scott Melton, Kelly Land's boss, about it. I told him God wanted me to cash out on September 12 and that I would be giving Kelly Land a call. When Kelly and I spoke over the telephone, I sensed Scott, a Christian, had spoken to her about me. I found Kelly to be exceptionally kind and positive. She said she hoped everything worked out for me. I could sense she, too, was a believer.

When I went into the office to sign the paperwork the following week, I instantly recognized Kelly as the "smiling woman" in a dream the Lord gave me on December 24, 2004! In that dream, I became an overnight multimillionaire by something being metered. (Crude oil pumped from the ground or gasoline pumped at a service station is metered.) The smiling woman in my dream was quite happy for me. She was not at all surprised by my sudden turn of fortune. She smiled broadly and knowingly, while all the other spectators looked on completely shocked.

Chapter 14
Prophesying to Israel's Old Dry Bones

While I waited for God to produce the funds to drill, He put another critical piece of the puzzle into place. His desire was to ignite a spiritual movement. The oil would back it. But more importantly, He needed to revive the inheritors of the trust. They needed new life breathed back into them, so He arranged yet another divine setup.

August 29, 2005

The Key to Reviving Israel's Old Dry Bones

At the end of our praise session yesterday, Pastor Tims at New Destiny welcomed all first-time visitors. "Nice to see you all here on this last Sunday of the month of August ... as we move into the September, the ninth month of the year, the birthing month."

Already on my feet with tears streaming down my face from our time of praise and worship, I lifted my head and hands to heaven and began to speak in a heavenly language, a rarity for me. Soon I was really sobbing.

I could not contain my tears of joy. Although I was not a first-time visitor, I knew that special welcome was for me! I would officially give birth to The Ephraim Project when we drilled our first well next month.

Pastor Tims then introduced a guest pastor, who traveled all the way from London, England to bring us a Word from the Lord. No one knew the message he would bring to us that morning, not even Pastor Tims. When he asked us to turn to Ezekiel 37, I was confident God sent him to speak to me about Ephraim, to talk about God's revival of Israel's old dry bones!

The visiting minister told us there were many layers of revelation in Scripture, which I knew to be true. He warned he was about to take us to a much deeper level than the average Christian was used to. He started by telling us there was a connection in Scripture between "bones" and "promises."

He gave several examples—from God fulfilling His promise to Adam to give him a helpmate by producing Eve from his rib bone; to the children of Israel taking Joseph's bones to the land God promised them when they left Egypt; to God not allowing the Roman soldiers to break Jesus' bones after He was crucified. That would have represented a broken promise.

From there, he turned his attention to the focal text of Ezekiel. The Lord promised to reunite Israel's descendants whose bones were scattered in the graveyard of the nations into one house and under one Head. That seemed like a promise, long dead.

Nevertheless, if God made such a declaration, He would keep it. It did not matter how hopeless or unachievable the promise seemed. The current state of affairs is of no consequence to God. If God said it, He will do it. He is a Promise Keeper.

The speaker suggested that maybe God's promises had not been fulfilled in our lives because we had neglected to prophesy. Perhaps, we had failed to speak, by faith, the thing or matter into a manifested state under the inspiration of the Holy Spirit. He used Ezekiel's example.

God told Ezekiel to prophesy to Israel's old dry bones. Ezekiel prophesied and bones—scattered throughout a valley—began to rattle. The bones united "bone to bone." Sinews came upon the frame and then flesh and skin. Ezekiel prophesied again, as God commanded, and breath came into them. Now they were alive! Suddenly, the whole house of Israel appeared on its feet as "an exceedingly great army."

The Lord promised Ezekiel He would one day "open the graves" of His people and bring them back into their land, a united house under one King, the Messiah. As the pastor taught, I suddenly had a revelation regarding a dream God gave me seven years earlier. In the dream, I was a young version of the Prophet Ezekiel. I was a precocious little girl and I happily introduced myself to everyone as Ezekiel: "Hi, my name is Ezekiel!"

"Get Ezekiel on the Line!"

Scripture teaches God does nothing among His people without first revealing the matter to His prophets (Amos 3:7). As I listened to the pastor, I knew God was giving me revelation on how He was going to fulfill His promise to revive and reunite Israel at the end of days. He was giving me a key—a key to unlock Ezekiel's prophecy, spoken thousands of years earlier. I knew it was time for the old dry bones (promises) of Israel to live! And I was the Lord's Ezekiel! I could hardly wait to get home to see what God would tell me next. He was waiting for me when I burst through the door!

That very day, the Lord had me record in my journals exactly what He told Ezekiel to prophesy. Then, I crafted seven "Thus saidth the Lord" statements that would begin to fulfill the ancient words spoken by Ezekiel. After that, I found two long dry sticks of approximate equal length. I wrote on each stick exactly what God instructed Ezekiel to write.

Next, I identified seven days at the end of August and beginning of September, when I would march three times around the grounds of my rambling complex, fittingly called "The Preserve." I combined the two long sticks and carried them with me as one on my seven-day march. During those seven days, I proclaimed, decreed, and declared to the listening heavens and earth everything God said would come to pass. I did not care who saw or heard me. I must have looked crazy to those who passed me. But I was confident my every move was orchestrated by the Lord!

August 29, 2005

Tearing Down the Walls

Yesterday, I began my "Jericho Walk." I marched around the entire Preserve, prophesying what God had revealed to me over the years about the mission and purpose of The Ephraim Project and how it related to the reunification of the 12 tribes of Israel. I resolved to walk around the complex declaring the Word of the Lord on the matter at least three times for seven consecutive days. I implored the Lord to bring down any and all walls—spiritual or temporal—that would keep His people from being revived and seizing His promises.

In Ezekiel 37, God told the Prophet Ezekiel to prophesy:

1. *"O Dry Bones, hear the word of the Lord! Thus says the Lord to these bones: 'I will cause breath to enter into you, and you shall live. I will put sinews on you and bring flesh upon you, cover you with skin and put breath in you and you shall live. Then you will know I am the Lord'" (vv. 4-6).*
2. *"Come from the four winds, O breath, and breathe on these slain, that they may live" (v. 9).*
3. *"Behold, O My people, I will open your graves and cause you to come up from your graves, and bring you into the land of Israel. Then you will know I am the Lord" (v. 12).*
4. *"Surely I will take the stick of Joseph, which is in the hand of Ephraim, and the tribes of Israel, his companions; and I will join them with it, with the stick of Judah, and make them one stick and they will be one in My hand" (vv. 19-20).*

5. *"Surely, I will take the children of Israel from among the nations, wherever they have gone, and will gather them from every side and bring them into their own land; and I will make them one nation in the land, on the mountains of Israel, and one King shall be king over them all; they shall no longer be two nations, nor shall they ever be divided into two kingdoms again…." (vv. 21-22).*

For seven consecutive days, three times each day, I declared and decreed as the Lord's Ezekiel of the last days:

Thus says the Lord God …

1. *"It is a new season for the descendants of Jacob, the house of Ephraim and the house of Judah." (Based on "A New Season" prophecy, given by Dr. Paula White, on August 20, 2000 in Honolulu, Hawaii.)*
2. *"Let the 'new thing' I have planned for this set and appointed time 'spring forth.' It is time to give birth to the 'new thing' I have ordained." (Based on Isaiah 43:18-21.)*
3. *"It's time to put flesh on the 'old dry bones' of the whole house of Israel. I say, 'Live!'" (Based on Ezekiel 37.)*
4. *"Denny's stock will rise to a level on September 12, 2005 that will fund the drilling of oil for The Ephraim Project." (Based two prophetic dreams the Lord gave me.)*
5. *"I will open a door of hope for Jezreel (scattered seed of Jacob) in the Valley of Achor/Trouble." (Based on Hosea 2:15.)*
6. *"I go before Ephraim to make the crooked places straight, to break in pieces the gates of bronze and cut the bars of iron. I will give Ephraim the treasures of darkness and hidden riches of secret places, that people may know I am the Lord." (Based on Isaiah 45:2-3.)*
7. *"I will answer Jezreel (scattered seed of Jacob) by commanding the heavens to command the earth to deliver up its treasures of grain, new wine, and oil to Jezreel in the last hours of the last days to spread the Gospel of Yeshua Ha'Mashiach across the earth." (Based on Hosea 2:21-23.)*

Solving the Mystery of the "ZZZ"

At the half-way mark on the first day of my march, I noticed a series of Zs painted on the pavement in big red letters. I saw three Zs, side-by-side (i.e., ZZZ). They appeared to be construction or irrigation markings of some sort. I saw three sets of them in succession.

When I spotted the letters during earlier walks, I made no connection between them and my Ezekiel call. This was despite the Lord calling me Z—short for Ezekiel—since 1998! It was not yet time for me to make the link.

But when I saw the markings on my dry-bones walk, God finally opened my eyes. Now the ZZZ symbols made *perfect* sense! I could not stop marveling. God had gone before me. He put the Zs there for the march! I cannot explain the fierce faith that filled my heart when I made the connection. With every step, I was completely, utterly confident that I was on a divine march, orchestrated by heaven and everything, absolutely EVERYTHING I prophesied would come to pass. I had NO DOUBT, NONE!

The AntZ Connection

When I made the connection between the Zs and my march, I also laughed out loud, because just a few days earlier I had been talking to the Lord about how much my life seemed to mirror that of the character "Z" in the animated film, *AntZ.* Let it be known, I am like a little child and I *still* love cartoons! Unless we change and come to Christ as little children we will not see His kingdom (Matthew 18:2-3).

"Z" was such a misfit and a dreamer. He continually questioned and challenged the status quo. But the peculiar rebel, who marched to the beat of a different drum, ended up foiling a wicked plot to destroy his colony.

At the time, I asked, "By the way, Ishi, why is he named Z?" It seemed like such a weird, random moniker. The Lord revealed the significance of his name on my "dry bones" walk. He explained, like Z in *AntZ* and the Prophet Ezekiel—I would end up, one day, sounding an alarm for others to heed.

Lessons from AntZ

After that revelation, I could not wait to watch *AntZ* again. I did that very evening. That little animated cartoon had a lot to say about the twisted world-system we find ourselves in today:

1. Our present world is the wicked construction of Satan, the "prince of this world."
2. It reduces people to insignificant possessions.
3. It is based on a vast web of lies, deceit, and deception.
4. It oppresses people, making them slaves.
5. It labels and categorizes people, deliberately causing class divisions and splits.
6. It seeks to maintain artificial hierarchies that divide people into groups and categories. The divisions cause tension, aggression, even hatred. Divided, people are more controllable, manageable.
7. It says, "Everyone has a place. Don't move out of your place. Don't cross that line!"
8. It cannot satisfy or bring lasting happiness to anyone, even those who have the most esteemed roles.
9. It calls the individual to sacrifice for the good of whole, based on fraudulent principles.

10. It hates individualism. Individualism often breeds rebels, insurgents. The individual matters only to the extent that he or she can serve the system. When that ceases to be the case, the person becomes expendable.
11. It does not like thinkers. If a person thinks too much, he or she might expose corruption. Thinkers upset the status quo. However, it is good to be a thinker, a dreamer even, to imagine better ways, to have new ideas.
12. Most people are compliant to the system and easily duped.
13. Most people dance to the beat of the majority. It is just easier.
14. When the dissenter breaks free from the system, it is difficult for the person to understand and negotiate his or her new world. But eventually, the rain stops, and the person sees clearly. God makes a way.
15. It is unwise to follow orders blindly. (Avoid: "I have my orders!")
16. Many people have power and authority from above, of which they are not aware. They must learn to use it! (Z: "Stop digging on your own authority!")
17. Mutineers will find trouble. (Z: "Trouble is my name.")
18. System buckers will not always know what to do. They must move by faith. (Z: "Don't worry! I know *almost* exactly what I'm doing!")
19. A catastrophe is brewing just underneath the surface, involving many world leaders; they are being inspired by the spiritual underworld. The rest of us must help one another to "get out" before we all die.

20. A person must die to self (or literally) to truly live and save others entangled in Satan's web.
21. Have "apple-pie-in-the-sky" hopes. As impossible as everything seems, God will uproot and demolish the corrupt establishment and all those who are wedded to it!

I completed my "Jericho Walk" within the seven allotted days, and then I waited for God. I knew my proclamation to revive the old dry bones of Israel had set things in motion within the unseen spirit world.

Chapter 15
Fighting the Good Fight of Faith

After completing my time of prophesying, I waited for a drilling rig to become available. I prayed the funding would appear before the rig. Just as I instructed, Kelly Land cashed out my stock options on September 12, 2005. I needed $471,000 to drill. God gave me $469,800! Scott Melton told me it was a wild roller coaster ride!

He explained that as soon as the broker tried to sell my stock, I became entangled in a stock RUN DOWN! "Ray, just as they tried to cash you out, the stock plummeted!" I knew that was the enemy trying to thwart God's plan to fund the drilling.

I was on an airplane, unreachable by phone, when Scott made the executive decision not to cash out the third package, despite my explicit instructions to liquidate all three no matter what. (I was happy he made that decision!) It was as though God wanted to see if I would follow His orders to the bitter end. When I did, He intervened at just the right moment.

Combining the $469,800 with the $1,300 in my savings account, I had exactly enough to drill with no excess. I had hoped for a surplus so I could climb further out of debt, but that was not God's plan. I had no other money in the world except my monthly paycheck. In fact, I did not have the money to pay taxes on the cash I had just received. I refused to worry about it. God would take care of it. I was simply grateful and humbled to invest all that I had to save souls.

As God would have it, the unavailability of drilling rigs pushed the drilling start-date back several times to October 13, 2005. We started to drill at 6 p.m. that day at sundown. Later, I realized God's hand was in the timing. Days after we began, Rabbi Kokeb reminded me that October 13, 2005 was Yom Kippur, the Day of Atonement. It was the most sacred day on the Hebrew calendar. And it began at sundown.

The drilling ended right at the completion of Feast of Tabernacles, 14 days later, on October 27, 2005. Feast of Tabernacles is another important fall feast on the Hebrew calendar. The timing could not have been more appropriate since the oil trust was for the house of Ephraim! Clearly, God was behind the scenes, synchronizing every detail, according to His all-wise plan.

I was not prepared for what came next.

"What?" I could barely hear John through the static on the line.

"You discovered brine!" John repeated. Brine is salt water. He later estimated the output to be about three thousand barrels a day. That's 1.1 million barrels of brine a year!

What a colossal letdown! What a HUGE disappointment to our entire family! It flew in the face of everything God had revealed to me—the dreams, the visions, the revelations ... HIS VERY WORD! How could this be?

This is how the disciples must have felt to see the Man they had walked with for three and a half years, hanging on a cross. Did He not heal the blind? Did He not cause the lame to walk? Did we not see Him feed the hungry multitudes, calm the seas, raise Lazarus from the dead? He spoke with such power and authority. He said He was the Son of God!

I could just hear the thoughts whirling in their minds? *What happened? Were we all duped? Worst, are we crazy?* It made no sense. It did not add up. Yet, hanging on that cross was *exactly, precisely* where Christ was supposed to be, according to God's infinite wisdom.

A conundrum. That is what I had on my hands, a conundrum. Like the disciples, I would have to wait on God. Against all rational thought, I trusted He would make sense of everything in time.

I did not know it at the time, but in the wilderness, where I was at this juncture of my life, I had to trust God wholly, solely, completely. I could not rely on the reports of men or even what my own five senses told me. I found great solace in the fact that I obeyed God without understanding.

I looked crazy in the eyes of family, friends, colleagues, and others. But I knew I was in the middle of something I could not understand, and therefore, could not explain with my finite mind. God would reveal more at the set and appointed time. Until then, I had to keep obeying and pressing my way through whatever the days would bring.

Believing I had discovered brine, despite all God had previously shown me, I tried to find a market for it. After He blocked my three attempts to sell the well to interested buyers, I tabled the project. The Lord turned my attention to other matters.

The Founding of The Ephraim Project

On July 18, 2005, three months before we began drilling, I founded a ministry, The Ephraim Project, to serve the most impoverished among us, first abroad (Ethiopia, Liberia, and Haiti) and then stateside. God intended the well to support the private foundation. I knew that from the beginning. But at that time, I wrongly assumed the Foundation would primarily be involved in awarding grants to evangelical, Christ-centered ministries to further the Gospel. I discovered later that God intended to be far more intentional in directing the funds to Ephraim's tribes for that purpose. I also wrongly assumed the well's proceeds would begin funding grants right away. God had other ideas.

His first priorities were to build the fledgling ministry... *and* to transform me in the process! I would not see a dime of that trust until He had thoroughly overhauled my life. I did not know the mess I was in His eyes. While I loved Him and His Word, I maneuvered through life more like a child of the world than a child of God—just like His corporate bride. We both needed to be completely, totally overhauled. We were *not* ready for the Bridegroom. Christ is returning for a bride without spot or blemish.

The Lord tore down my old life and rebuilt it from scratch! After having made millions of dollars as a corporate executive, I had to learn what it was like to live on the lowest rung of society, to thrive and prosper at the nation's poverty level. In God's all-wise plan, I needed to become one of the "least of these" to serve them as God would, with a heart of mercy and compassion. He also desired to build my faith and confidence in Him as an Ever-Present Help. I learned *not* to "go down to Egypt" for *any* kind of help *ever*! The Lord would be my sole Source, henceforth and forever.

I did not know when I founded the ministry that God would lead me to give up virtually every possession I had. He took away every crutch except Himself. I did not know I would become homeless and completely reliant on His miracles and on the mercy of the good people He put in my path to assist me. But I did. And I flourished! I grew and blossomed just as He intended and so did The Ephraim Project. The Lord made every day an adventure!

As of this printing, the ministry has been serving Orlando's poor and homeless for six years with stunning results. We have fed and clothed countless multitudes and have helped remove scores of families from Orlando's streets. God graciously allowed us to restore dignity and worth to many who had lost all hope.

After the private foundation was established in July 2005, we changed the name of the drilling enterprise from The Ephraim Project to Ephraim Oil and Gas, LLC. Shortly thereafter, John Manners died of a sudden heart attack. He had worked with me for more than three years to help drill our well. He also endeavored to help me find a market for the brine. I was in Ethiopia, trying to bring humanitarian aid to the Ethiopian Jews there, when I learned of his death in an email. I simply did not know what to think.

Chapter 16
"It is Oil!"

Twenty-two months after capping the well, right at the time The Ephraim Project inaugurated Project NewStart®, our ministry to Orlando's homeless families, the Lord began to unveil the mystery surrounding the well.

I had, indeed, struck oil! But God's plan for it was far beyond anything I could have possibly imagined!

He began the unveiling with a sermon message. It was during that message I came to realize my personal destiny was inextricably tied to the oil trust, but the trust was inextricably tied to a time of great judgment on the United States and the world! The oil would be released during a time of grave disaster. Until then, the well would remain capped.

August 26, 2007

"Take Another Look"

Today, a guest pastor spoke on behalf of Pastor Tims, who will be undergoing surgery later in the week. I heard God speaking to me through the pastor's message. He took his text from Revelation 5:1-7.

In the text, the Apostle John wept bitterly because no one in heaven, on earth, or under the earth was worthy to open the scroll and loose the seven seals of judgment. No one was worthy to even look at it. So he wept.

An angel appeared and told John to take another look. He said, "Do not weep. Behold!" The Lion of Judah, the Root of David, who prevailed on earth to cover the sins of all mankind, stepped forth out of the midst of God's throne. He was worthy to open the seal of the scroll for earth's title deed belonged to Him. He paid for it with His blood.

The pastor also likened each of our lives to a scroll (or book) that represented our destiny. Each of our scrolls contained many promises of God, yet to be revealed. Our destinies were etched and sealed inside the scroll, ready to be revealed at the appropriate time. Until that time, we were to wait patiently on God's promises. We were to fight on ... press ... pursue ... persevere.

The speaker stressed that some of us had been persevering for years, and still we found ourselves no closer to what God promised. I thought of the well. Suddenly, everything he spoke seemed to fit my life: "People, who started out later than you have now surpassed you," he said. "It looks as though God's promises to you will never be fulfilled." He offered: "Wipe your eyes! Take another look!"

He explained there were some situations in which prayer, fasting, studying the Word of God, praising, worshiping, singing, dancing, listening to tapes, and attending conferences would not move us one inch farther in the fulfillment of our destinies. They were good practices, and we should do them, but they were not the answer to our breakthroughs.

"Sometimes nothing short of a divine intervention from God Himself will do. Yes, sometimes, the Lion of Judah Himself must step into your situation to break the seal that will take you to the next level, to bring to pass what God has promised."

By this time, my ears were like antennas! I was utterly confident God was speaking to me! For years, the Lord told me, "You will be raised up in the judgment." That statement must be recorded in my journals more than 100 times. But I never understood what it meant. Later, He told me on several occasions, "You are a seal! Your life is a seal!" This was even more perplexing than the first declaration.

When the Lord first began saying I would be raised up in the judgment, I often thought ... raised up from where and for what? Now, as I sat in that pew, I suddenly understood. The release of the oil was tied to my destiny in some way, and both were connected to a time of judgment ... the breaking of a seal!

The Lion of Judah, the Root of Jesse held the key. The devil was not holding me back. What was happening to me (or not happening) was not about the devil. It was about the season. Destinies are tied to seasons. Old seasons end, new ones begin, all under the divine hand of God. My destiny was in God's hand. In due season, He would unlock my tomorrow and take me to the next level.

On October 18, 2007 at 1:31 a.m., after three days of fasting, in the quiet of my bedroom, I heard a Voice whisper to me. Although I was asleep, I distinctly heard in my spirit: "Take another look!" My eyes popped open. I knew the Lord had spoken and I knew His words pertained to the well!

Minutes later, I remembered "Take Another Look!" was the title of a sermon I'd heard two months earlier. I jumped out of bed to find my notes on the sermon. I had recorded them in my journals. As I studied my notes, I realized with sudden clarity I would not see a drop of oil until Christ broke a judgment seal. In Revelation 6, 7, and 8, the Lord opens seven judgment seals. The breaking of one of those seals held the key to my own personal breakthrough. When it is broken, I will experience the personal release—the breakthrough—I have waited for, for so long. My release will not occur one nanosecond before the breaking of that seal.

After this realization, the Lord sent other people to me to confirm that I had, indeed, struck oil. It was not brine. That is why He consistently blocked my negotiations to sell what I thought was a brine well!

The Lord revealed this truth to six people—three men and three women. One of the most remarkable things about this unveiling was of the six of them, only two knew each other. However, the crux of the Lord's message to me from all six was the same: "You struck oil! Don't give up!"

First, the Lord spoke to two of the women separately. Then, he spoke to the three men separately. Lastly, he spoke to another woman. Neither of the first two women He spoke to knew I had been involved in the drilling of a well. I had kept the enterprise secret from many of my associates and friends. As a result, these women who knew nothing about my drilling a well were very reluctant to speak to me about it. Perhaps, they misunderstood what the Lord was telling them. Following is the exchange I had with one of the women, Susan Mamboleo:

October 20, 2007

Susan Mamboleo's Dream: "It is Oil!"

On Monday, October 15, we started a 21-day fast at New Destiny. The church is facing some problems, so Pastor Tims called for a corporate fast. Clearly, something is wrong, but we have not yet been told what's brewing. I decided to use the 21 days to also pray and fast about the well, sitting dormant for nearly two years.

The following day, I went to the home of my missionary friend, Susan Mamboleo, to pray. She and her husband, George, are native Kenyans. They work for Campus Crusade for Christ and live close to my neighborhood. God put it in my heart to visit Susan and pray for her family's finances. They have their three children in college and they struggle to make ends meet.

The Mamboleos had been such a blessing to me, and in return, I wanted to bless them. More than anyone else I have ever met George and Susan demonstrate daily what it means to live by faith. They have so little, yet they are so generous with what they have. I have seen them travel to the other side of the world for Christ, visiting several countries without even a dollar in their pockets! They are a powerful couple in the Spirit and a delight to watch.

During my visit with Susan, the first thing I learned was she was also on a 21-day fast from food. She started her fast the same day I started mine. She made me a cup of tea and we both found a place to sit on her living room floor.

After about 30 minutes of just catching up on our families and ministries, she said: "You know, I had a dream about you. I woke up, and I almost called you that night, but I didn't. It was about your oil well."

I was momentarily stunned. "My oil well?" I managed to ask with emphasis on the word oil. How did she know I had a well?

"Yes, God gave me a dream about your oil well." She didn't miss a beat. "I saw your oil. What I saw, Ray, was as black as this table." She reached over and tapped her black lacquer living room table for emphasis.

"I saw it shoot up suddenly from the ground. It was jet black and went high in the air. Then the Lord said to me, 'Tell Ray, not to give up. It is oil!'"

Susan confessed she had the dream two weeks earlier but did not want to tell me. George kept prodding her to call me, but she did not know what the well pertained to, so she kept quiet. She thought I would think it was all foolishness.

I sat there dumbfounded. I could not speak. Not only did Susan not know I had drilled a well, she did not know that I had been told I had discovered brine (salt water)! Now, here she was refuting what I had been told. The Lord told her to tell me: "It is oil!"

Three months after Susan shared her dream with me, I learned through my friend, Donald Bain (now deceased) that oil would be released through an "underground explosion." He saw the explosion in a dream he had on January 27, 2008.

His dream was one of the most dreadful ones anyone has ever relayed to me about myself. "Ray, my dear, you were in a fight you could not win," he told me. "You were surrounded!" My stomach knotted. In the dream, he stood high on a cliff, looking down. He described the scene:

> *You were on a rickety, bamboo bridge that swayed back and forth. You had a sword in your hand, and you were fighting. These flying reptiles were attacking you from the air. Alligators and snakes were in the water below, waiting for you to fall through cracks in the bridge.*
>
> *There was a sound. Everything stopped. Everyone looked up. The sky opened. Something like stardust fell from heaven. It fell on you, the bridge, and through the bridge. It fell on the water, pass the alligators and snakes. Deep down, it went. Then suddenly, there was a huge explosion—an explosion of oil!*

Donald's dream made my stomach flip and for good reason. Jeri, my best friend, introduced me to Donald more than 20 years earlier when she and I lived in Miami. The three of us became good friends. When Donald was filled with the Spirit, he had an incredible prophetic gift.

Over the years, I heard him prophesy to people with amazing specificity. Many cried, even wept, because he often hit a private cord. He relayed details to them that only God could have revealed. It happened to me on a number of occasions.

As unpleasant as it was, I knew his dream would come to pass. At some point, like Israel, I would be surrounded by hostile forces I could not beat. Heaven would have to intervene. The result would be the release of oil for Ephraim *and* judgment for the nations of the world.

Chapter 17

The Coming Disaster and the Woman in Revelation 12

On March 14, 2008, God revealed to me that the underground explosion Donald saw in his dream on January 27, 2008 was an earthquake! But it was no ordinary quake. Heaven released something. In the dream, stardust fell to earth and split open ("exploded") earth's foundations and delivered oil.

I have come to suspect that the "stardust" in Donald's dream symbolized Satan and his angels being cast from heaven to earth after losing a battle with the Archangel Michael and his angels (Revelation 12:7-9). Per Revelation 12:13-14, it seems after Satan's expulsion there could be a three-and-a-half-year period for God's Josephs to evangelize a crippled world in turmoil, using the oil trust. When Satan and his fallen angels are given the boot, the cosmic disturbances are so cataclysmically jolting that the world is thrown into a mayhem and an upheaval it has never before experienced (Isaiah 13:13, Isaiah 24:17-18, 21, Isaiah 34:4, Revelation 6:12-16).

In the ensuing days, months, and years, the Lord gradually revealed to me another shocking bit of news. There was an inextricable link between the global disaster, the woman in Revelation 12, and the rapture.

Revelation 12:1-6 introduces the woman in Revelation 12. As discussed in Book One, *The Spotted Bride*, the Scripture passage is a layered. It points to more than one fulfillment:

> *Now a great sign appeared in heaven: a woman clothed with the sun, with the moon under her feet, and on her head a garland of 12 stars. Then being with child, she cried out in labor and in pain to give birth. And another sign appeared in heaven: behold, a great, fiery red dragon having seven heads and 10 horns, and seven diadems on his heads. His tail drew a third of the stars of heaven and threw them to the earth. And the dragon stood before the woman who was ready to give birth, to devour her child as soon as it was born. She bore a male Child who was to rule all nations with a rod of iron. And her child was caught up to God and His throne. Then the woman fled into the wilderness, where she has a place prepared by God, that they should feed her there one thousand two hundred and sixty days.*

The woman in the passage is actually two different women, symbolizing Israel at two different points in history more than 2,000 years apart. Both are believers in Christ as Messiah. Mary, the mother of Jesus Christ, symbolizes Israel *before* the commencement of the Church Age. She gives birth to the Child who will rule the nations with a rod of iron (v. 5a). That Child grew up to be Jesus Christ.

The second woman symbolizes Israel at the *end* of the Church Age. She bears a second child, whom the Antichrist will try to devour at the end of the age. However, God catches up the child to His throne (v. 5b). This child is not Jesus Christ. He is the Lord's son, Joshua. Jesus was never snatched up to God's throne as a baby! (See Book One, *The Spotted Bride* or *Joshua, the Prince* for a fuller explanation of the child.)

Based on Acts 1:3, 40 days after His resurrection, Jesus Christ, our Lord and Savior, ascended into heaven. His disciples witnessed His ascension. Fifty days later, He sent the Holy Spirit to indwell His followers, inaugurating the Day of Pentecost. He now sits at the right hand of God, the Father, as our King and High Priest. He will return as earth's Judge, and afterward, rule as Messiah.

God catches up the second woman when He takes the child. They are caught up together. She does not flee to the desert after giving birth. I am the woman who is caught up. I am Joshua's mother. God has made it abundantly clear to me through numerous visions, dreams, and other revelations that I will be taken with Joshua as a sign to His corporate bride that she will follow. She, too, will be caught up to heaven at a time when the entire world is sinking in utter bedlam.

Our snatching up is her assurance she will go too, to reassure her the rapture is not a myth. Many will think it is because they expected the Church to be taken before this point. They were wrong. The bride needs to be cleansed and purified. Christ returns for a spouse without spot or blemish. The body *must* match the Head. And she will after He is done.

The woman who escapes to the wilderness[11] to a place prepared by God for 1,260 days (v. 6) is not a literal woman. She is metaphorical. She is a remnant of Jews (and perhaps others of Hebrew descent) who flee the Antichrist during the Great

[11] Wilderness could be symbolic of an arduous, barren period or literal.

Tribulation. She also represents Israel. God will preserve her for Himself. She will come to know Christ as Messiah during this horrific time of judgment as He nurtures and protects her away from the dragon. Micah 5:3 reveals that this remnant will be reunited with the rest of Ephraim at the age's end.

The snatching up of the child and his mother heralds the Great Tribulation, which will last three and a half years or 1,260 days. It is a time when God allows the Antichrist to ensnare the entire world. This period will culminate in an all-out, global assault against the present-day Jews of Israel and all believers in Jesus Christ. Afterward, God will then pour out His fury on the wicked.

The Flood

According to Revelation 12:16, the Lord causes the earth to open to help the woman in Revelation 12. That is, He sends an earthquake to help the woman, whom the serpent-dragon (Satan) tries to drown with a flood:

> *So the serpent spewed water out of his mouth like a flood after the woman that he might cause her to be carried away by the flood. But the earth helped the woman. And the earth opened its mouth and swallowed up the flood which the dragon had spewed out of his mouth (Revelation 12:15-16).*

The Lord has given me numerous dreams in which I am overtaken by flood waters. For years, I thought a day would come when I would nearly drown before God plucked me from rising waters. (Epic flooding could happen when devils are cast to earth, and they rupture earth's foundation and trouble its seas.) However, I have come to realize that I may also be engulfed by a deluge of ungodly attacks on my character, ministry, and life. The onslaught, orchestrated by Satan and his minions (i.e., flying reptiles, alligators, and snakes in Donald's dream) will come from popular culture, liberal media, and those wedded to this present world because of the end-time message I reveal to the body of Christ (and the world).

Repeatedly, the Lord has shown me instances in Scripture, in which a flood also refers to something that overwhelms. It can be an invading army overrunning a nation's borders or waves of trouble consuming a person's life (Jeremiah 46:7-8, Isaiah 8:7, Daniel 11:10 NIV, Amos 8:8, Amos 9:5). When God rescues me from the flood, the world will be sinking under the weight of ungodliness. He interrupts my attackers. He quiets scoffers, mockers, and naysayers with an earthquake.

A Prototype Rescue

Years ago, the Lord gave me Psalm 18—His rescue of David from "many waters"—as a prototype of my own deliverance. In Psalm 18, the Lord bowed the heavens to come down to help David against the attacks of King Saul. Saul saw David as a threat to his throne and dynasty. As a consequence, a raging tide of ungodliness rose against David; he could not become what God intended—a ruler over His people— because of the ungodliness. The Lord plucked David from the flood of ungodly assaults perpetrated by the king and others. Since David's foes were too strong and too numerous for him to defeat, God came down to settle the matter.

When the Lord came to David's rescue, He came with an earthquake. I believe he will do the same in my case: *"The earth shook and trembled. The foundations of the hills also quaked and were shaken because He was angry" (v. 7).* He also opened the foundations of the earth and released a (literal) flood of His own!

> *The Lord thundered from heaven, and the Most High uttered His voice ... then the channels of the sea were seen, the foundations of the world were uncovered at Your rebuke, O Lord, at the blast of the breath of Your nostrils (vv. 13a, 15).*

The Lord also came in dark clouds, in thundering and lightning:

> *He bowed the heavens also, and came down with darkness under His feet ... He made darkness His secret place; His canopy around Him was dark waters and thick clouds of the skies ... He sent out His arrows and scattered the foe, lightning in abundance, and He vanquished them (vv. 9, 11-12a, 14).*

The Breaking of the Sixth Seal

Scripture passages Revelation 12:1-6 and Revelation 12:12-16 seem to dovetail with another important passage of end-time Scripture—Revelation 6:12-16. In Revelation 6:12-16, a massive earthquake jolts the planet:

> *I looked when He opened the sixth seal, and behold, there was a great earthquake ... and every mountain and island was moved out of its place. And the kings of the earth, the great men, the rich men, the commanders, the mighty men, every slave and every free man, hid themselves in the caves and in the rocks of the mountains, and said "Fall on us and hide us from the face of Him who sits on the throne and from the wrath of the Lamb!"*

We learn from the next verse (v. 17) that the quake inaugurates the Day of the Lord, a time of God's wrath on the ungodly, as foretold by several Old Testament prophets (e.g., Joel, Amos, and Zechariah): *"For the great day of His wrath has come and who is able to stand?"* Thus, the Day of the Lord commences with the breaking of the Sixth Seal. A super-quake is released, but is this the same quake mentioned in Revelation 12:16? I believe it is.

We should note that the preceding five seals are the result of human activity. They are simply precursors to the Dreadful Day. However, God intervenes directly with the breaking of the Sixth Seal. He rocks the earth off its axis.

After supernaturally sealing His army of 144,000 Hebrew evangelists (Revelation 7:1-8), the Lord breaks the Seventh Seal (Revelation 8). It is highly probable that God will use the mega-quake to galvanize these troops, to resurrect them from the "graveyard of the nations." These are the "old dry bones of Israel" that the world presumed long dead (Ezekiel 37).

The Seventh Seal unleashes seven trumpet judgments (Revelation 8-9, 11:15-19). The seventh and final trumpet judgment unleashes yet another seven bowl judgments (Revelation 16). The 21 judgments culminate in Christ's return (Revelation 19).

A Fateful Birthday!

On a number of occasions, the Lord indicated to me He will intrude in earth's affairs in such a way that it will strike terror in the hearts of earth's residents. But in May 2010, He added a new twist. He connected His frightful intrusion to my birthday! He hinted that day will be on the anniversary of my birth!

May 24, 2010

A Coming Rescue and Release

On Sunday morning, the first thing the Lord put in my hand was a prayer I received from Consecrate Orlando. On Pentecost Sunday, the prayer will be prayed worldwide by Christians in 220 nations. I began to read the prayer out loud to the Lord. When I came to the part, "Lord Jesus Christ, You alone are worthy to open the scrolls of history …." I paused. I could not go on.

Immediately, Revelation 5 came to mind. In Revelation 5, an angel told Apostle John to stop weeping, to take another look. There was only One worthy to open the scroll—the Lamb of God. The Lord Jesus Christ came forth to open the scroll that loosed seven seals. Those seven seals unleashed 21 judgments upon the earth.

God has told me repeatedly that I will be raised up in the judgment. He also told me numerous times that I was a seal, that my life was a seal. This meant He had to personally break a seal on my life before I could be raised and released. Surely, Donald's dream of me being attacked and the breaking of this seal on my life are related!

In the margins of my Bible, where David talked about the floods of ungodliness making him afraid (Psalm 18:4), I had previously scribbled: "Revelation 12:16." I cannot remember when I made the notation, but obviously, I connected Psalm 18:4 to the flood the woman in Revelation 12:16 would experience. Just before reading Psalm 18 this morning, having read it countless times before, I asked the Lord to show me something new.

Suddenly, something in the notation grabbed my attention! Why had I not noticed it before? I blurted: "12:16? Lord, that's, that's … my birthday!" Immediately, I turned to Revelation 12:16. I made a surprising discovery. Although I'd read the verse many times before, I was taken aback. For the first time, I realized that my birthday tied to a flood and an earthquake.

In Revelation 12:16, God opens the earth (i.e., sends an earthquake) to swallow a flood. Satan (referred to as a serpent in verse 15 and a dragon in verse 16) will try to drown the woman in Revelation 12 with a deluge of flood waters. But God opens the earth to swallow the torrent spewed by him.

The verse indicates when I can do no more against Satan's flood of attacks and tidal waves of ungodliness surround me, blocking my call and making me afraid, God will cause an earthquake to consume Satan's assaults. The earthquake will cause many who are ungodly to pause and assess their lives. Perhaps at that same time, the Lord will unleash Ephraim's oil, just as Donald saw in his dream.

Interestingly, an earthquake struck the United States more than 200 years ago. The earthquake of 1811 was named the New Madrid Earthquake. It happened along the New Madrid fault line in the Midwestern region of the country.

At a 7.7 magnitude, it was the largest recorded earthquake in the United States. Although the shaking was felt throughout the entire nation, Arkansas, Missouri, Mississippi, Illinois, and Tennessee experienced the greatest land damage. Most interestingly, however, is that the earthquake occurred on the anniversary of my birth, December 16!

In addition to that curious fact, I saw calamity ("911") in the year of that quake, 1811. The sum of 8 and 1 equals 9; the 9 juxtaposed to 11 creates 911, the number for disaster. Also, according to Ed F. Vallowe's *Biblical Mathematics—Keys to Scripture Numerics*, 11 is the number for divine judgment and chaos[12] while the number nine represents finality or divine completeness from the Lord.[13]

Was the 1811 earthquake a shadow of a larger one to come, one that will occur on the anniversary of my birth?[14] More than a year after the birthday revelation, the Lord gave Andre, my former husband, a short, curious dream about my birthday. In

---

[12]Ed F. Vallowe, *Biblical Mathematics—Keys to Scriptural Numerics*, The Olive Press, 1998, pp. 94.

[13]Ibid., p. 88

[14]*The anniversary of my birth does not occur until I reach the exact moment I was born on December 16, 1953. I do not know the exact time because the hospital records no longer exist, and both of my parents have passed away.*

his dream, clearly there was something significant about the day of my birth to the nation.

July 20, 2011

Andre's Dream: Ronald Reagan's Birthday Wishes

This morning Andre relayed a strange dream to me. In his dream, he and I were giving an intimate garden party among friends. We lived in a small place that had a miniature garden. It was the day before my birthday, December 15.

Suddenly, Ronald Reagan, the late former President of the United States, appeared at the door: "Happy Birthday, Ray!" I thanked him for remembering my birthday.

Andre responded, "That's nice that you remembered her birthday, but you are one day too early." Reagan responded, "I knew it! I knew it! I thought her birthday was December 16, but Nancy said it was today, and she is usually right about those things."

Andre offered to turn our little garden party into a birthday celebration, but Reagan told him not to. "We will celebrate her birthday tomorrow," he said. He turned and left. The dream ended.

I cannot recall ever dreaming about Ronald Reagan or anyone else telling me that he or she had. Reagan's presence in Andre's dream is significant. Andre admired Reagan as did many Americans, especially conservative Christians. I gleaned three points from the dream:

1. The former president's presence in the dream suggests my birthday is of some importance to the United States. Why else send a president?
2. The dream also implies my birthday and whatever happens on that date cannot be observed a day too early. Whatever happens is for a set time.

3. Reagan being in the dream hints that my birthday will mark a time of celebration for conservative Christians in the nation, those whom popular media negatively refer to as the religious right. Since Reagan came to commemorate my birthday, people with spiritual values akin to those of the former president would perceive my birthday as something to note.

The dream only strengthened my conviction that another earthquake could hit the nation on the anniversary of my birth. The second national quake will swallow up a flood of ungodliness. In fact, the Lord has revealed to me through several dreams (and the dreams of others) that many people will come to know Christ as a result of an earthquake. On March 28, 2013, He further corroborated this truth:

March 28, 2013

Speaking Through an Earthquake

I woke up this morning making two strange declarations. I simply repeated what I heard refraining in my spirit: "The Lord speaks through the earthquake" and "I heard His Voice in the earthquake."

"Ishi, what am I talking about?" I asked when I was fully awake. Suddenly, I remembered a vision He gave me earlier in the night. In it, I saw a massive zigzag rupture in a large slab of concrete.

Upon remembering the vision, I realized many people will come to know Christ as their Lord and Savior because of a devastating earthquake. That was the reason many heard the Lord "speak through the earthquake" or "heard His Voice in the earthquake."

The Significance of December 16th

I have come to believe that a mega-quake inaugurating the Day of the Lord will occur on some future December 16th. Putting aside every dream and vision the Lord has given me that suggest an earthquake will occur on the date of my birth—some I have not shared in this book—the Lord showed me something very peculiar one day in Scripture that sealed December 16 in my heart as the fateful day.

One day, while studying my journal notes on Revelation, something jumped out at me. I had not noticed it before. I saw my birthday linked to all three Revelation passages that the Lord had given me to study! I did not notice the pattern earlier because He gave me the passages in stages. But after I recorded them together on a single page, I caught the odd pattern. *What are the chances of that?* I asked myself. My birthday, December 16, can also be rendered 12/16 or 12-16.

Revelation Passage	What Happens
12:1-6	Mystery of the woman, child, and dragon; child snatched up to God's throne as dragon seeks to devour child; dragon and his angels are thrown to earth. A remnant of Jews (and Hebrews) preserved in the wilderness for 1,260 days.
12:16	God opens the earth (i.e., sends an earthquake to swallow the flood the serpent-dragon spewed at the woman to drown her).
6:12-16	The Sixth Seal broken; causes a mega-earthquake; commences the Day of the Lord .

Revelation ***12:1-6*** discusses a woman giving birth to a special child, whom the Antichrist seeks to kill. The child (and literal woman) are snatched up to God's throne, while a remnant of God's people flees into the wilderness for 1,260 days to be preserved by Him. These events mark the rise of the Antichrist and the start of the three-and-a-half-year Great Tribulation.

Revelation ***12:16*** recounts how God opens the earth (i.e., sends earthquake) to help the woman, whom the dragon (Satan) seeks to drown with a flood. The quake in this passage is quite possibly the same one that comes with Christ's breaking of the Sixth Seal!

Revelation 6:***12-16*** vividly describes a colossal earthquake being unleashed by the Lord when He breaks the sixth judgment seal. The breaking of this seal initiates the dreadful Day of the Lord, the Great Tribulation follows closely behind.

As alluded to earlier, related to the breaking of the Sixth Seal, the eruption of a mega-quake, and the snatching up of the male child and his mother, is yet another significant event. As insane as it sounds, Satan and his legions of fallen angels are booted from heavenly realms, to earth!

> *And war broke out in heaven: Michael and his angels fought with the dragon; and the dragon and his angels fought, but they did not prevail, nor was a place found for them in heaven any longer. So the great dragon was cast out, that serpent of old, called the Devil and Satan, who deceives the whole world; he was cast to earth, and his angels were cast out with him (Revelation 12:7-9).*

The Day of the Lord is a time when God judges *all* rebellion, in heaven and on earth (Isaiah 24:21). At that time, the *powers* of the heavens—Satan and his fallen angels—will be shaken, banished from the celestial and atmospheric heavens. Their expulsion from the heavens will shake the nations of earth—the lands and the surrounding seas (Haggai 2:6-8, Matthew 24:29, Hebrews 12:26-27). This may cause massive flooding everywhere; tsunamis could easily flood coastal areas. It is possible that cosmic disturbances (e.g., falling asteroids, meteors) will accompany their expulsion.

Further pointing to the heavenly shaking and expulsion of devils are Revelation 12:4 and Revelation 6:13. Revelation 12:4 states, *"the dragon's tail drew a third of the stars of heaven and threw them to earth."* This means one-third of all the angelic beings who mutinied with Satan against God are finally cast out of heaven during the Day of the Lord along with their leader.

In Scripture, angels are frequently referred to as "stars" or "starry hosts" (e.g., Job 38:7, Judges 5:20, Psalm 33:6, Nehemiah 9:6, Daniel 8:10-11, Daniel 12:3, Revelation 1:20, Revelation 9:1-2). Hence, the term "stars" in the Revelation passages can be literal *and* metaphoric. They can refer to literal stars *as well as* Satan and his cohorts' ejection from the heavens.

Could it be sometime after these fiends are flung to earth that Satan incarnates the "man of perdition" or the Antichrist? Thus, Satan's heavenly eviction triggers the Day of the Lord, which instigates the Great Tribulation. The Antichrist rises to power during this time.

Isaiah 24:17, 18b-21 (NIV) also refers to Satan's celestial removal and the distress it brings to earth. Satan, working in and through the Antichrist, ensnares the entire world:

> *Terror and pit and snare await you, O people of the earth. The floodgates of the heavens are opened, the foundations of the earth shake. The earth is broken up, the earth is split asunder, the earth is thoroughly shaken. The earth reels like a drunkard, it sways like a hut in the wind; so heavy upon it is the guilt of its rebellion that it falls—never to rise again. In that day, the Lord will punish the powers in the heavens above and the Kings on the earth below.*

The Antichrist Revealed

I have no doubt President Barack Hussein Obama is the future Antichrist. I stake my life on it! Satan could incarnate him some time after he and his angels are hurled from heavenly realms and sent to earth. On July 7, 2012, the Lord gave me a dream in which I was to deliver a message to Obama. The message: "The meek shall inherit the earth." On January 5, 2013, I awoke to His Voice saying, "You have a prophecy for the President of the United States." That same month, on January 29, God revealed to me in an "Ides of March" dream that an assassination attempt would be made on Obama's life. Ides of March pertains to a specific day on the Gregorian calendar—March 15, 44 BC—when the Roman Emperor, Julius Caesar, was assassinated by the Roman Senate. The senate feared the king, who sought to be "dictator for life" and began to fancy himself a god, would destroy their republic with his tyranny. It led to mayhem and civil war.

On February 6, 2013, the Lord gave me yet another dream in which I was told to tell Obama that the least in the kingdom of heaven is greater than even John the Baptist, who in heaven's eyes, was one of earth's greatest men. He also said to tell Obama, *"From the days of John the Baptist until now, the kingdom of heaven has been forcefully advancing, and forceful men lay hold of it."*

Two months later, on April 2, a Voice announced to me upon waking, "The Antichrist will be revealed." Two days after that announcement, on April 4, the Lord gave me a dream in which I saw Satan—cast as a two-horned, red reptilian creature of a man—flying in a swift chariot. He was on his way to earth! This was a preview of his eviction!

In a dream six days later, on April 10, I saw Obama suffer a fatal head wound! He was surrounded by men wearing blue windbreakers. They were ATF (Alcohol, Tobacco and Firearm) agents. After he was shot, Obama morphed from a man into a hideous, growling beast. The man-fiend resembled an upright furry bear with hollow, dead eyes. It held a long assault rifle in its left hand, an indication that it was a beast of war. I have no doubt who Barack Hussein Obama is going to be in the future. I must refer the reader to Book Three, *The Late Great United States*, for the theological discussion of this topic.

The people of the United States gave "the little horn" his crown. It was just a beginning. He will grow in popularity and worldwide stature. It is my belief that somehow during his august political career, Obama will rise to lead a conglomeration of nations, a form of the present United Nations. This will make him perfect prey for a satanic incarnation. After Satan incarnates the popular leader, Obama will become earth's supreme ruler, the Antichrist.

The Walls Come Down

The Lord revealed to me that the giant quake will devastate critical infrastructure throughout the U.S. It will also affect other parts of the world. It will be a global event. The world's present banking system, led by the U.S., will be destroyed. Perhaps, this will pave the way for the Antichrist's new system of trade and commerce, in which people will be required to take his mark to buy or sell.

Walls will fall as they fell in the days of Joshua. Just like the walls of Jericho toppled, the walls of the U.S. and other nations—spiritual *and* temporal—will collapse. In the days of Joshua, the city of Jericho kept God's people from entering the Promised Land, so God brought down its walls. For the same reason, He will crumple our walls. He will bring down economies, systems, and infrastructures. He will do what He must, to get our attention. When our fortifications give way, many people will turn to God.

Great numbers of people will look to God for deliverance. They will come to know Him in a genuine way, as He hears and answers their cries. They will no longer look to themselves, to others, or to human government for their provision, protection, or preservation.

Anything that keeps God's people from seeing, trusting, and depending on Him, will be judged an idol. God will remove all idols. Only when the idols are taken away, and people turn to Christ, can they inherit the ultimate Promised Land ... heaven!

The Lord will release crude oil during this tumultuous time to underwrite an unprecedented move of His Spirit. The Josephs will play a pivotal role in leading a spiritual movement that will eventually explode worldwide. Many people will be "saved alive!" These souls will be ushered into God's kingdom at the time of the rapture. I will be taken, along with the child, *before* the Church as a sign to her that she, too, will soon be removed. At that time, without spot or blemish, she will welcome the assurance that her Bridegroom will soon remove her from an imploding planet. (I may not be present to oversee the full execution of the oil trust, but God will raise up who He needs to complete His work.)

Should a destructive earthquake shake the country on a future December 16th as the one did on December 16, 1811, the Lord will have given us *two* witnesses. God always establishes a matter with two or more witnesses (Deuteronomy 17:6, 19:15, John 8:17). He will have confirmed what I have written to His bride is true. It is not a fairy tale or the delusions of a deranged woman. His people will do well to heed the warnings and prepare. Christ is returning for a bride without spot or blemish. She must WAKE UP! REPENT! AND COME OUT OF MYSTERY BABYLON! If she does not, she will share in her plagues!

Epilogue
One Moment in Time

At the end of October 2011, about two months after Pastor Zachery Tims' death, the Lord began to speak to me about how Ephraim must seize and maximize the critical moments at the age's end, to make them count for all eternity. We must take hold of our "moment in time." He began with a film called *In Time*.

October 29, 2011

A Modern-Day Parable: In Time

As I watched the film, In Time, *I sensed the Lord speaking to me. The film was a modern-day parable. The Lord often speaks to me in parables, so I watched intently. At the film's beginning, I felt a single pronounced birth pain and grabbed my stomach. At other points in the film, I cried because I saw my own life, that of my family, and others I knew.*

The movie put forth what, at first, seemed like a strange premise. What if we lived in a time and place where time is the ultimate currency in which everyone deals? Time is money. In such an economy, the more time you have, the richer you are, and therefore, the more life you can buy. Likewise, the less time you have, the poorer you are, and the less life you have because you spend all your time trying to stay alive. And what if the system is rigged so that the rich steal time from the poor to live longer? The system increases rates and quotas so that the poor never catch up or get ahead.

The film reminded me of how life is for the poor black and Latino masses in the United States of America. The top one percent of Americans controls the clear majority of the nation's wealth and they rigged it that way. This privileged class of citizens have managed to use its vast wealth to manipulate markets, media, government policy, public opinion—even our educational system. Thus, over the past 30 years the rich have become richer and the poor, poorer. The American Middle Class has gone the way of the dinosaur.

The only difference between the U.S. and the imaginary nation in the film was the rich in the film became immortal because they stole so much time from the poor. The poor died at age 25 unless they could get more time on their clocks. Consequently, the rich were like immortal gods.

A man named Will, acting bravely one night on behalf of a stranger, is given the gift of more time by the stranger. The gift is bestowed upon him unexpectedly. The stranger also tells Will a secret: The system is rigged to steal time from the poor and give it to the rich, thereby creating a form of slavery. The truth is there is enough time for everyone if some did not hoard it. Few of society's time-poor could break free from the destructive scheme. The rich, on the other hand, lived well and forever.

Will has lived in the system 28 years, In the toughest area, Time Zone 12 (ghetto), where people kill for a week. He knows all too well how hard it is to earn time to live. Until he meets the stranger, his life is consumed with trying to earn enough time to stay alive. He has time for little else. He lives day to day, rushing through life, trying to get more time.

Although he always seems to be just about out of time, Will is generous with the time he has, sharing his minutes and days with people who have less than he. He is deeply moved by people who perish in the streets because they run out of time. This eventually happens to his mother.

Unbeknown to Will, he is very much like his father who was killed when Will was a little boy. He was slain for earning time and giving it away. Giving time away upsets the system. It disrupts the status quo.

Before the stranger clocks out, having transferred more than 116 years to Will as Will slept, he asks the young man for only one thing. He scrawls his request on a windowpane: "Don't waste my time!" In other words, He gives Will a trust and asks him not to squander it.

Will resolves he will do something useful, good with the gift of time he has been given. He will make it count. The giver of the 116 years is a type of Savior because his gift of time to Will ignites a revolution. Although the stranger dies, he helps save many people.

Immediately, Will decides to infiltrate the other side. He enters the time-rich world that is deftly cut off from the time-poor zones. (It can cost a person two years to cross a single time zone.) The time-rich live as if the time-poor do not exist. They close their eyes to the plight of the time-impoverished, yet they buy into a system that steals time from them daily so they can live longer.

Will quickly discovers how the other side lives, if one can call what they do living. The ones rich in time dwell in constant fear of someone stealing their time. They conduct highly controlled, guarded lives. They are careful not to do anything too dangerous to abruptly end their lives. So, they never undertake anything of real consequence.

On the other hand, Will, who knows what it is like to live on the edge of time, is fearless. He ventures much. This is a clear advantage he has over those rich in time or anybody invested in the present system.

Will is soon joined by a female partner from the time-rich side, whose eyes are opened. She comes to believe in his cause. Together, they begin to steal time from the rich and give it to the poor. In doing this, they disrupt the established system that, in turn, upsets the Timekeepers.

The Timekeepers are the establishment's enforcers. Their careers are devoted to maintaining the status quo, keeping the system as it is, although the established order is clearly corrupt. They ignore thugs in the street who prey on the poor to steal their time. The thievery of thugs maintains the conventional order.

Will and his girlfriend become outlaws. A bounty is placed on their heads. Becoming outlaws does not stop the couple because they are not vested in the system. They are not greedy, and do not want any more time for themselves other than what they need to fulfill their purpose. Their goal is to transfer some of the time (wealth) of the elite rich to the poor masses.

They become modern-day Robin Hoods. The more they transfer, the more empowered the poor become until the people who are formerly slaves to time begin to break out of their time zones. The people begin to experience life as it was intended for all.

"Don't Waste My Life!"

On February 25, 2012, four months after seeing the film, I received a rather startling report about how New Destiny Christian Center had changed after Pastor Tims' death. New Destiny-East, a satellite church on the eastside of Orlando, started by him, closed. Many who attended the main church in Apopka left. Under Pastor Tims, the Apopka location used to have two packed services. During special conferences, people standing in the hallways were herded into ancillary rooms to join the congregation via television.

At one point, Pastor Tims planned to build a larger sanctuary. The main sanctuary was too small for all the congregants. Now the report was that only the first five rows were filled. Dr. Paula White, the new pastor, sat on the platform with her two children. New Destiny was a different place.

That day, the Spirit began to speak to me about a special moment in time that had passed. What New Destiny was, and is, is God's business. The Lord needed the former New Destiny to exist when it did to birth The Ephraim Project and other ministries. He raised up Pastor Tims and his wife, Pastor Riva, to start New Destiny Christian Center in Apopka, Florida.

At the same time, in another city, He was revealing Himself to me in extraordinary ways and starting me on the strangest of expeditions with Him. It was a journey of great wonders. He saw then that I would need the ministry he was birthing in The Tims, to birth mine. He called Pastor Tims and his family from Baltimore to Orlando, where He would eventually call me.

The Lord introduced me to Pastor Tims, a Will Smith lookalike, in a dream in August 2002, three years before I ever met him. In due course, I lived the dream. The Lord pulled me out of Corporate America to serve the "poorest among us" through The Ephraim Project. And just as the dream revealed, the transition from a wealthy businesswoman to the head of a local ministry that offered no monetary compensation frightened me out of my wits. But Pastor Tims appeared in the dream (and in real life) to help me make a smooth shift.

During my four years at New Destiny, God showed up *every* Sunday during the worship service and *every* Thursday night for the church-wide Bible study to speak mind-transforming realities to me. Through Pastor Tims, He spoke truths that made me detach from everything in the world and follow Him to an utter end of myself. In the process, The Ephraim Project was born. Other ministries were incubated just that way at New Destiny as well.

I will be forever grateful to Pastor Tims and Pastor Riva for how they allowed the Lord to use them. Their sacrifice opened an entirely new destiny for me (and others). In the dream, Pastor Tims delivered me to my present place of ministry. I know the Lord will use The Ephraim Project to spark a spiritual revolution that will touch millions.

It appears we two—Pastor Tims and I—were in a relay race. After handing me the baton to run my segment of the race for God's glory, he died. One of the very last photographs taken of him shows him in a fedora. I had never seen him in a hat before, much less, photographed in one. The snapshot struck me as odd the moment I saw it on the cover of a magazine in a doctor's office. He appeared to be going somewhere in that hat. Within a month, he was dead. God had taken him home.

Pastor Tims' ministry was for one moment in time. It lasted 15 years. That is exactly how long it took the Lord to get me from the start of my strange journey of wonders to the head of a fledging ministry. He used Pastor Tims and New Destiny to help me get there.

In September 2009, the Lord called me to leave New Destiny. I did not want to go. I could have stayed forever or so I thought. The call out of New Destiny was sudden, unexpected. I did not know that one Sunday I would never go back. God blocked my few attempts to return. I also did not know Pastor Tims would be dead in less than two years. God simply told me, "It's time to go," and He used the story of Rahab the prostitute to get me to leave New Destiny and join St. George Orthodox Church.

Rahab was not married to her past. She shifted when God presented her with the opportunity to do so. She recognized her season at Jericho was about to end. She aligned herself to God's plan. Because she was willing to let God write a new chapter in her life, Rahab ended up in the genealogy of Christ. The Rahab sermon would be one of the last I would hear Pastor Tims preach because I obeyed God's command to leave.

Eventually, St. George became my new church home, and after a while, I settled into the rhythm there. God opened my eyes to new things. As I glanced back at New Destiny, I saw it gradually morph into something else. It will never be what it was under Pastor Tims, and God does not want it to be. It was meant for only one moment in time. Under Dr. Paula White, the Lord will turn New Destiny into something else special for His glory. I pray for her success.

In a dream on September 15, 2007, God showed me Pastor Tims being struck in the spirit realm for my cause, for the sake of The Ephraim Project. At the beginning of the dream, God showed New Destiny, under his leadership, birthing many life-changing ministries. The Ephraim Project was one.

At the end of the dream, a demon-possessed young man—clearly getting his instructions from the underworld—entered a retail electronics store that sold all manner of weird television sets. I was there with my daughter, scrutinizing the store's wares. Suddenly, the young man walked over to us and raised his arm high to strike me. At that very moment, out of nowhere, Pastor Tims popped up in the dream. He stood between me and the possessed man. He took the blow.

Shortly after the dream, a scandal broke at New Destiny. Based on my dream and other revelations the Lord has given me, I remain convinced that what happened to Pastor Tims was inspired by witchcraft and sorcery. He had become a special target of the underworld because of the compelling ways God used him. The scandal marked the beginning of the end for Pastor Tims and New Destiny, as I had experienced it. God's servant had succumbed to Satan's wily schemes and attacks. He was taken out of the race.

Nevertheless, before he left, he prepared the way for me and others just like John the Baptist prepared the way for our Lord. And, just like John the Baptist was removed after our Lord entered His public ministry, the Lord removed Pastor Tims after he helped establish me and others in our public ministries. It was our turn to run the next leg of the race.

As I pondered Will's name in the movie *In Time,* I could not help but liken Pastor Tims, who could be Will Smith's twin, to the stranger who bequeathed 116 years of time to Will. Just before he died, the stranger left a message for his unsuspecting heir: "Don't waste my time!"

Likewise, I can now hear Pastor Tims calling to me and others who sat under him, giving us a similar admonition: "Don't fritter away what I gave you! I poured all I had into you! My ministry gave you a new destiny and opened the way for the spiritually impoverished to enter God's glorious riches. Don't squander it! Grab hold of the moment!"

Just as Will in the film, *In Time*, ignited a revolution, God will use Ephraim and others to spark a last days' revival in America and around the globe. I have no doubt. It will be a significant part of my own moment in time before the close of the age. It will be a moment that will never come again. I (we) must make the most of the opportunity.

While a moment in time can last a person's entire lifetime in the eternal scheme of things, it is simply a dot, a speck, a footnote in the annals of time. One moment in time can be many millions of moments in real time. They can be the world's Camelot moments, a time when God allows something marvelous, wondrous to occur for His purposes and glory. One moment in time can apply to individuals, families, communities, nations, even civilizations.

Through books and documentaries, the Lord allowed me to glimpse the pomp and grandeur of the Egyptian, Assyrian, Babylonian, Medo-Persian, Greek, and Roman empires. Where are they now? Each had its moment in time—before it lost its luster and lure and was brought to ruin by a successor empire. Only Christ's Kingdom will last forever.

Abraham, Moses, Joseph, King David, the Apostle Paul, and Mary, the mother of Jesus Christ—all lived their moments in time. They left their imprints on the world and useful legacies for future generations. Ghandi, Mother Teresa, Martin Luther King Jr. had their moments as did Elvis Presley, Michael Jackson, and Whitney Houston. We will all leave an imprint. Something.

For the person living the moment, it can feel like an eternity. A person can feel he or she has reached that one special moment in time and nothing else could ever top it. Then they discover that moment in time was just a chapter's closing and another's beginning. There would be many more special moments to come.

Surely, Moses thought life could not get any better than being an Egyptian prince. Chances are as a young man he thought he would die a royal prince of Egypt. God had another plan.

Finding peace on the desert's backside with his soulmate and two boys, tending his father-in-law's sheep, would surely be how Moses would live out his days. There, in calm, isolated serenity, he would grow to be an old man. God had another plan.

Leading a nation out of Egypt after it experienced 430 years of slavery and besting the world's top ruler with many wonders surely would be the zenith of his life, his one moment in time. Little did Moses know, as he led the children of Israel out of Egypt, he would wander in the desert 40 years until God could get Egypt out of His children.

A person's moment in time can be pure drudgery. One can be oblivious that a mark is even being made on the world through his or her personal suffering. The mark the person leaves can be remembered for a generation or for many generations, even across millennia. It can teach something useful to one person or to millions, even billions of people.

The only way to live a moment in time is day by day, step by step, inch by inch—one moment at a time. One person's moment in time can intertwine with another's and others'... and together they give brilliant testimony to a magnificent, wondrous God, who orchestrates all moments in time.

No moment in time lasts forever. Moments in time fade away and die, making room for other moments. All moments fit God's glorious purposes. At some point, time gives way to eternity. Time is no more. Then we shall see what God has done with every moment in time for His glory. I trust we all will be delightfully surprised. Ephraim, this is your season! This is your time, your moment! Don't waste it! Seize it!

Appendix

Judah's Descendants—Idolatry Led to Their Return to Slavery During the Transatlantic Slave Trade

Moses prophesied the Hebrews would return to slavery on slave ships if they engaged in idolatry (Deut. 28:68). This occurred during the Transatlantic Slave Trade when their descendants were taken on slave ships to the New World. Although Ephraim was scattered to nations by the Assyrians in 722 B.C. and the Judah was taken captive by the Babylonians in 586 B.C., the people were never taken on slave ships because Israel shared the same land mass as Assyria and Babylon. Released by the Persians after 70 years, the exiles used the same/similar routes to return from Babylon. When the Romans scattered the Judeans in 70 A.D., many migrated south to Egypt and across sub-Saharan Africa to Africa's West Coast. The migration took approximately 1,200 years. Before being enslaved again, Hebrew progeny helped build the pagan empires of Ghana, Mali, and Songhai. When God fully restores Israel, reuniting Ephraim and Judah under Christ Messiah, they "will come trembling from the west" (Hos. 11:9-10).

Lift Every Voice and Sing

James Weldon Johnson, 1871 - 1938

Lift every voice and sing,
Till earth and heaven ring,
Ring with the harmonies of Liberty;
Let our rejoicing rise
High as the list'ning skies,
Let it resound loud as the rolling sea.
Sing a song full of the faith that the dark past has taught us,
Sing a song full of the hope that the present has brought us;
Facing the rising sun of our new day begun,
Let us march on till victory is won.

Stony the road we trod,
Bitter the chast'ning rod,
Felt in the days when hope unborn had died;
Yet with a steady beat,
Have not our weary feet
Come to the place for which our fathers sighed?
We have come over a way that with tears has been watered.
We have come, treading our path through the blood of the slaughtered,
Out from the gloomy past,
Till now we stand at last
Where the white gleam of our bright star is cast.

God of our weary years,
God of our silent tears,
Thou who hast brought us thus far on the way;
Thou who hast by Thy might,
Led us into the light,
Keep us forever in the path, we pray.
Lest our feet stray from the places, our God, where we met Thee,
Lest our hearts, drunk with the wine of the world, we forget Thee;
Shadowed beneath Thy hand,
May we forever stand,
True to our God,
True to our native land.

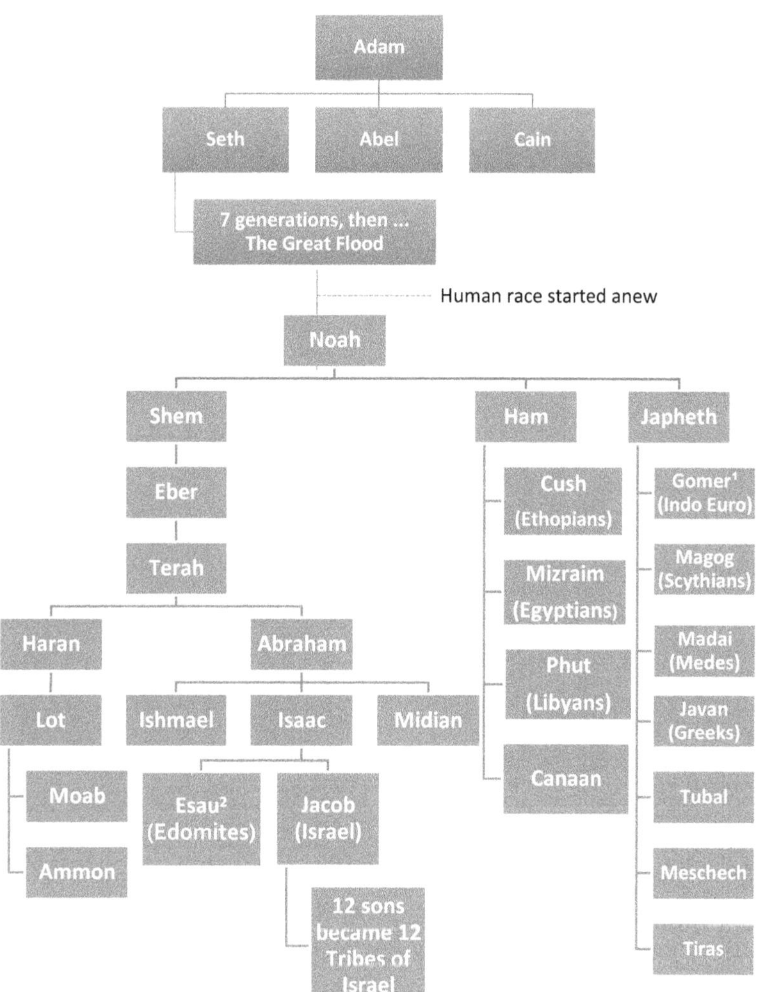

Lineage
Adam to Jacob (Israel)

[1]The Ashkenaz people, who represent approximately 80% of the Jews living in Israel today, trace their lineage to Gomer, a descendant of Japheth, not Shem. According to Genesis 10:2-5, the Ashkenaz are identified among the "coastland peoples of the Gentiles." They must have converted to the Hebrew faith at some point in history since the original Hebrews/Jews are descendants of Shem through Abraham, the Patriarch of the Hebrew faith. [2]Although descendants of Shem, Sephardic Jews, who represent nearly 20% of Jews living in Israel today, descended from Esau or the Edomites; they are not in the lineage of Jacob/Israel.

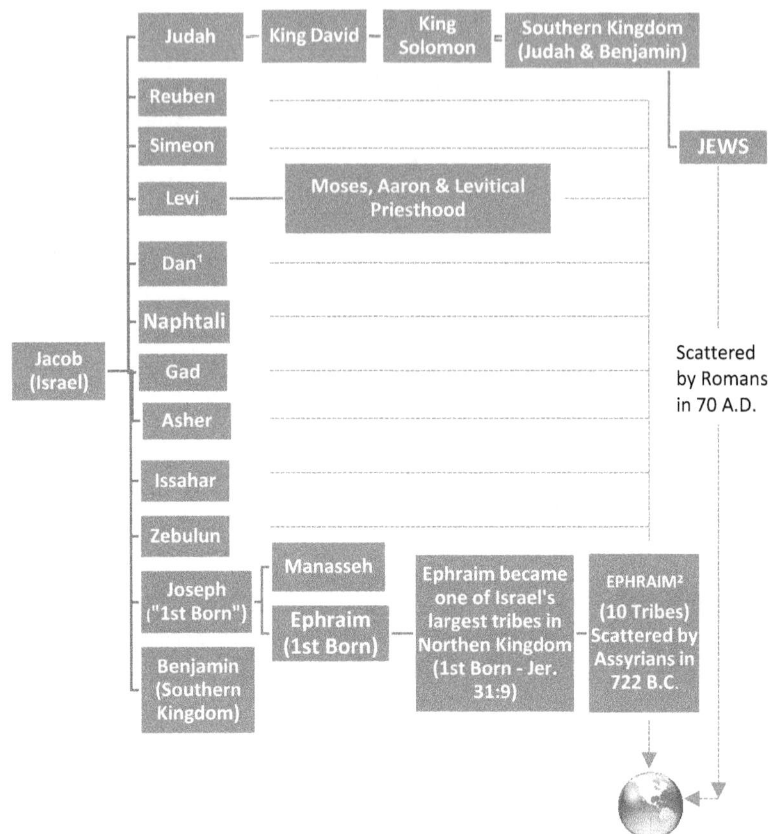

House of Ancient Israel
Dispersion of Ephraim and Judah to the Nations

[1]At the end of age, the tribe of Manasseh replaces Dan; Ephraim becomes Joseph; the two are synonymous (Rev. 7:6, 8; cf Num.1:17-46, Eze.15, 19). [2]Ephraim (10 "Lost Tribes") became a "multitude in the midst of the nations" or melo ha'goyim: "a fullness of the Gentiles" (Gen. 48:16, 19). Many descendants of the original Hebrews have been hidden within the Church since her inception; they have helped preserve the testimony of Jesus Christ for more than 2,000 years. As "Gentiles" with Hebrew roots (i.e., modern-day "Samaritans"), God will raise them up from the "graveyard of the nations" (from "old dry bones") at the end of the age for His glory (Eze. 36 and 37, Hos. 14:4-6, 8, Isa. 59:20-21, Jer. 33:7-9, Rev. 7:4-8). Presently, the descendants of the original Hebrews (Judah and Ephraim) are people of many colors and nationalities. The progeny of Ephraim, hidden within the Body of Christ, remains God's firstborn. They have the God-granted right, authority, and responsibility to oversee the spiritual and financial trusts of His family.

GOD'S TWO WITNESSES IN THE EARTH
EPHRAIM & JUDAH

EPHRAIM[1] **(10 Tribes)**	**JUDAH (Judah & Benjamin)**
NEW COVENANT (GRACE) Jesus Christ is Messiah	**OLD COVENANT (LAW)** Reject Christ as Messiah *(Blinded until the "fullness of the Gentiles has come in" (Rom. 11:25-26)*
ORIGINAL HEBREWS (incl. JEWS) (Globally Dispersed) ▪ Many colors, many nations	**CONVERTED JEWS** (Living in Today's Israel) ▪ Ashkenazi (80% Pop.) ▪ Sephardic (20% Pop.)

Many of their descendants are hidden within the Body of Christ in Gentile nations, unaware of their Hebrew roots. They are part Hebrew and part Gentile (i.e., modern-day "Samaritans").

The Great Tribulation

Preserved and raised up by God as great witnesses for Christ Messiah at age's end. (Jer. 31:31-37; 33:7-9; Eze. 36:24-27; Eze. 37; Isa. 59:20-21; 60:1-3; Hos. 14:4-6, 8; Rev. 7:1-8)

A remnant will be saved *after* the Great Tribulation when the nations of the world turn against Israel under the 3½-year reign of the Antichrist. The remnant's desperate cry of repentance in the desert will trigger Christ's return. (Zech. 12:10-11; 13:8-9; Rev. 12:6, 14)

Both reunited under Christ

[1]*Jacob (Israel) prophesied that Joseph's seed, through Ephraim, who was designated as firstborn, would become "a multitude in the midst of the nations" or melo ha'goyim: "a fullness of the Gentiles" (Gen. 48: 16, 19). Ephraim became one of Israel's largest tribes. In time, the name Ephraim became synonymous with Israel's 10 tribes. The 10 tribes were scattered to the nations by the Assyrians in 722 B.C., where their descendants remain to this day, preserved by God. The Judeans' final dispersions to the nations occurred after Christ's ascension, in 70 A.D. and 135 A.D.*

www.ingramcontent.com/pod-product-compliance
Lightning Source LLC
LaVergne TN
LVHW012332100826
845148LV00017B/2119